THIS IS IT!

A START IN
INFORMATION TECHNOLOGY

Anne Ramkaran • Ian Ithurralde

Hodder & Stoughton

A MEMBER OF THE HODDER HEADLINE GROUP

British Library Cataloguing in Publication Data

Ithurralde, Ian
  This is IT!
  I. Title II. Ramkaran, Anne
  004. 0712041

ISBN 0 340 61104 9

First published 1995
Impression number   10 9 8 7 6 5
Year   1999 1998 1997

Printed in Hong Kong for Hodder & Stoughton Educational, a division of Hodder Headline Plc, 338 Euston Road, London NW1 3BH by Colorcraft Ltd.

Contents

Introduction

■ *How to use this book*

This book is intended primarily for students following the National Curriculum Information Technology programmes of study at key stages three and four. It will also prove useful if you are following skills-based courses for GNVQ. Whether you are taught IT as a specialist subject, or you are set tasks in other subject areas, and whatever hardware or software you're using, there are some design skills which you need to learn, and some methods which work better than others. This book will show you how to produce effective IT solutions to problems and, by looking at various applications of IT, will give you an insight into the wider aspects of the use of IT and its impact on society.

You are not expected to sit down and read the whole book, or even to read the chapters in order. Each main type of package you are likely to need to use has at least one chapter devoted to it. When you have an IT task to carry out, find the chapter you need and read it carefully. You will learn what you can expect the software to do and also how to approach the task to get the best results.

You will not find specific instructions for different software packages as there isn't room to cover all the packages available in one book. We suggest that you keep a notebook with a section for each package you use. As you find out the exact commands needed for that package you can write them down for easy reference.

Throughout the book we have stressed the importance of design. You will get the best out of IT work by doing the design work first, working through all the steps suggested. At the end of most chapters there is a list of suggestions for tasks you might try. Further tasks and worksheets are available in the worksheet and CD-ROM pack.

There are questions throughout the book. Some of these are examination questions, others are short questions within the chapters. Try to do these short questions as you come to them. They will show whether you have understood what you have read.

Each time a new technical term is introduced it appears in **bold** type. All these terms are explained in the glossary at the back of the book. We have tried not to include lots of technical detail about computer systems and software. If you want to know more you should read *This is IS!*, which covers all the additional work needed for GCSE Information Systems courses and gives you more detailed information on the medical, traffic control and supermarket applications of IT.

Information and Data

This picture gives us the same information as in the sentence – the cat is fluffy.

■ *What is information?*

Here is a piece of information:

The cat is fluffy.

This information tells us something about the cat. Information is always about something. It always has a **context**. If we take away the context the information loses its meaning. The word 'fluffy' on its own doesn't tell us anything.

PICTURES

We don't always provide information in words. The photograph on this page gives us the same information as the sentence above.

In some instances pictures can be more useful than words. For example, very young children can't read words but can learn to recognise pictures quite quickly.

GRAPHS AND CHARTS

Information can also be provided in the form of a graph or a chart. This can show important trends more clearly than a table of numbers. In Figure 1.1 the graph shows much more clearly that the average temperature is generally going up during this period than the table does, even though the line does go up and down a little from month to month. Always remember that presenting information like this can be misleading. You can make small changes look big, or disguise large changes by choosing the scales on a graph carefully.

A pie-chart (like the one in Figure 1.2) is a good way to show how

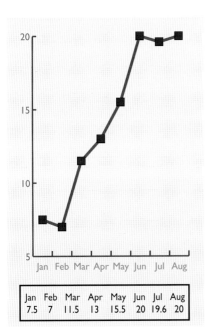

Jan	Feb	Mar	Apr	May	Jun	Jul	Aug
7.5	7	11.5	13	15.5	20	19.6	20

Figure 1.1 *The data presented in the table is much more meaningful if it is presented in a graphical form.*

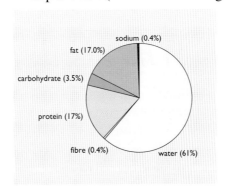

Figure 1.2 *Pie chart to show what goes into a beefburger.*

something is divided up. In this example we can see what kinds of food we get when we eat a beefburger, and what proportion of each kind we are eating.

SYMBOLS

Symbols can also be used to provide us with information. When we use symbols to get information across, we depend on the person who looks at them being able to understand the meaning of the symbols and interpret them correctly.

Look at Figure 1.3. These signs can give us information about roads, but only if we know what they mean. If we don't understand a symbol's meaning it provides no information to us. As long as we can understand them, symbols are a very good way of providing information quickly and effectively.

Figure 1.3 *The symbols in this figure can give us information about roads - but only if we understand them.*

SOUND

A great deal of the information we receive each day comes to us as sound – we are often told what to do, rather than being given written instructions. Your friends tell you where they have been and what they did. This kind of information is called **aural** information. It includes speech, music, and other kinds of noise.

Write down five different ways in which you can give information.

For each of these ways, think of an example where people use it in everyday life. Is there a particular reason why the information is given in this way?

Why are symbols sometimes used instead of words?

■ *What is data?*

Computers do not store information, they store data. Data has no context, it is just numbers and has no meaning until it is given a context. The computer can't think for itself. It doesn't know (and doesn't care) if the data it stores is correct for the use it's going to be put to – it is up to the user to make sure that the correct data has been entered and that they use it correctly.

A computer stores all data as **binary numbers**, which are made up only of ones and zeros. For example, it stores the letter A as the binary number 01000001. Binary numbers like this can be used to represent letters, other characters (like * % ! or <), numeric values, **graphics** or sounds.

Here are some examples of data items which could be stored in a computer.

47
Red
19/02/96
−456

Summary

Here the colour red gives us information.

- **Information** always has a **context,** and always has meaning for the person receiving it – for example the photograph on this page and Figure 1.4 contain information.

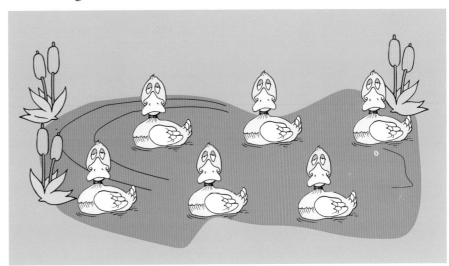

Figure 1.4 *Here the number six gives us information.*

- **Data** has no context and is meaningless until a context is supplied – 'red' and '6' are data.

SKILLS

When you have completed the work in this chapter you should be able to:

- Extract data from information.

- Work out what form of information to use for a task.

- Put data into a context.

Questions

1 Explain the difference between information and data.

2 Read this advertisement.

> **FOR SALE:**
>
> Four bedroom detached house in rural setting. Large landscaped gardens with fruit trees. £120,000.

Identify four data items that you might store in a computer file containing information on properties for sale.

3 Match these three data items to the contexts in the sentences below:

£8.56
100
Green

  a The computer has a hard disk which stores   megabytes.

  b The door of the house is painted   .

  c The bill for the meal was   .

For each data item, write a new sentence into which you could insert this item.

2 Handling Information

■ *Why use a computer to handle information?*

Information has always been stored in some way – until recently, in schools, hospitals, shops and offices, lots of information was stored on pieces of paper in filing cabinets. It's fairly easy to find one piece of information in a filing cabinet, but collecting together information to make lists is much more difficult and takes a long time. When we use a computer, the data stored takes up less space, and it is much easier to look things up. The computer can search the data it stores very quickly and can present the results of the searches in many different ways and print them out. This can make the information that has been stored much more useful.

Paper records in a health centre take up lots of space.

Patient records on computer take less space and are more convenient.

If health records in a hospital or health centre are stored on paper it's quite easy to find the record for one person. As you can see from the photograph there are lots of records, and to collect information on the age and sex of all the people suffering from one particular disease, for example, would mean that someone has to read the records of all the patients and copy out the information. This would require a great deal of effort and take a long time. If the health centre stored their records on a computer, a list of the information needed could be produced in only a few minutes. (You will find a detailed study of the information technology systems in a health centre in Chapter 14.)

■ *How does a computer store data?*

A computer can store a certain amount of data in its memory, but to store large amounts of data it has to have a **backing store**, where the data will stay even if the machine is switched off. The backing store is usually some kind of **magnetic disc**, although **magnetic tape** (stored on large reels) and **optical discs** (like compact discs) are also used.

A **database** is a store of data that the computer can read and process in a variety of ways. Getting the data out of the database and then putting it in context is called **information retrieval**.

The data in a database is organised into related **files**. Some databases have just one file, others have a number of files which can be linked together. A file is a collection of **records**, each of which contains data about one person or thing. The data in the records is separated into **fields**, each field holding just one item of data. Every field in a record has its own name, and to make things easier for the people using the database this name usually relates in some way to the field's contents.

You can see a summary of this information in Figure 2.1. As you can see, a database is not really very different from files in a filing cabinet – it's the way we can use the stored data which is different.

Q

What is a backing store?

Write down three types of backing store.

What do we mean by the term information retrieval?

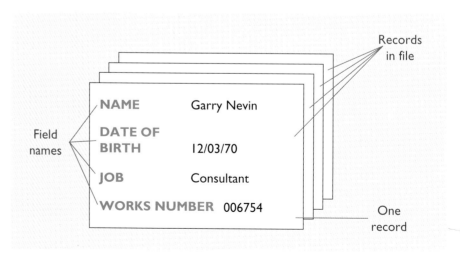

Figure 2.1 *In this diagram you can see how fields, records and a file are organised in a database.*

■ *How do we get information out of a database?*

To get information out of a database we have to **search** the file to find the records we need. (Some packages call a search a **query**.) We search by looking for a particular value in one of the fields. This value could be a word, a number, a date, a group of words or something else depending on what is in the field.

The database in Figure 2.2 is used by Ms Stillwell, who runs a small packaging supply business. Her customers order items and pay for them after they have been delivered. The file in this figure holds some details of the customer accounts – their names, customer number, and how much money they owe or have paid. You can see that these details are all stored in separate fields, called SURNAME, CUSTOMER __ NUMBER and BALANCE.

Customer number	Surname	Initials	Title	Balance	Area	Last order
0001	Smith	P.	Mr	-£233.56	04	27.04.94
0002	Ahmed	S.	Mrs	-£125.73	02	28.05.94
0003	Wells	P.J.	Ms	-£599.36	04	05.07.94
0004	Singh	V.	Mr	£2.65	01	19.05.94
0005	Lawrence	D.	Ms	-£45.50	03	10.03.94
0006	Bedford	L.	Mr	-£800.00	05	15.08.94
0007	Wilson	K.A.	Mrs	-£523.21	05	09.06.94
0008	Adams	H.T.	Mr	-£56.20	01	29.05.94
0009	Dhillon	K.S.	Mr	-£2.30	02	30.03.94
0010	Patel	V.N.	Mrs	-£264.21	02	29.06.94
0011	Braidwood	A.	Ms	£0.00	03	10.03.94
0015	Kramer	L.	Miss	£2.95	05	12.08.94
0016	Graham	J.	Mr	-£71.23	02	18.06.94
0018	Bates	T.	Mr	-£523.00	01	20.07.94
0019	Piejus	T.	Miss	-£350.00	05	30.07.94
0020	McFall	A.	Mr	-£605.85	03	19.08.94
0021	Penny	J.H.	Mr	-£695.20	03	14.08.94
0023	Smith	J.G.	Mrs	-£42.00	02	15.08.94
0025	Gallagher	I.D.	Ms	-£32.00	04	07.08.94
0026	Lee	M.	Mr	£56.00	04	23.07.94

Figure 2.2 *Part of the customer database used by Ms Stillwell.*

SEARCHING FOR ONE RECORD IN A FILE

If Ms Stillwell wants to find a single record in her file – perhaps to check how much Mr Bedford owes – she could search for the value Bedford in the field SURNAME. The search she would set up would be:

SURNAME = Bedford

This works well because there is only one customer called Bedford, but it wouldn't work if she wanted to find information

What is a primary key field?

Why are primary key fields important?

about Mrs Smith as there are two customers on her database called Smith. To be sure she gets just the record she wants she must search for a value which only that record has. She could find the record about Mrs Smith by searching for

CUSTOMER NUMBER = 23

because no other record has the value 23 in the field CUSTOMER NUMBER. Each record in this file has its own customer number, so by searching in this way she only extracts the one record she needs. A field that can be used in this way is called a **primary key field**.

SEARCHING FOR A GROUP OF RECORDS

One of the most useful things about a computer database system is that it is easy to extract groups of records which all have certain things in common. With a conventional filing system we couldn't do this without going through every record. When Ms Stillwell wants to send reminders to customers who owe money she can search the file for

BALANCE < 0

In other words, she's looking for all the records that have a value of less than zero in the field **BALANCE**, which shows that the customer owes money. She can use the records found as a result of the search to print individual reminders to pay.

The general pattern for a search (or query) command that you would use to find a particular record or group of records is:

(name of field to look at) (type of comparison) (value to look for)

You can use these types of comparison:

▶ **Equal to (=)**
To find all the records where the field contains the value to look for.

▶ **Less than (<)**
To find all the records where the field contains a value lower than the value given. This works for letters and dates as well as numbers, so for example A is 'less than' B and 02/01/94 is 'less than' 04/04/94.

▶ **Greater than (>)**
To find all the records where the field contains a value bigger than the value you have given. This works for letters, numbers and dates too, just like 'less than'.

▶ **Like (or sounds like)**
To find words that sound similar. This is good for finding names which sound the same but are spelt differently.

▶ **Contains**
To find words or phrases which have one part in common.

Some database packages use the symbols, others use words instead. Find out what comparisons your own database package can do and what symbols or words it uses.

SEARCHES BASED ON MORE THAN ONE VALUE

The computer can carry out complex searches based on more than one value very quickly. All the conditions that have to be met (all the values involved) are linked together with the words **AND** and **OR**. If Ms Stillwell wanted to mail adverts to customers who live in a particular area and who haven't placed an order in 1994 she could use the search

AREA = 4 AND LAST __ ORDER < 01.01.94

This search would select all the records of customers in area 4 whose last order was before 1 January 1994. The records could be printed out so that these customers could be mailed. Some database programs store dates as numbers. When they do this the date has to be stored in the order

year, month, day

so that searches can be carried out easily. For this kind of database 1 February 1994 would be stored as 940201 and any date before this would produce a lower number – for example, 3 January 1993 would be stored as 930103.

■ *What the database produces*

T he printout that you get from a database is called a **report**. You can produce a number of different reports from one database. A report can contain all the fields in each record, or just a few of them. It can be laid out so that it exactly suits the user's requirements. Some reports look like tables, with the field contents arranged in columns. In other reports the fields are spaced out over the whole sheet of paper. You can add headings and summaries of fields.

The report in Figure 2.3 includes five fields from Ms Stillwell's database file. The title (in this report 'Customers owing money') is a piece of fixed information which will be printed at the top of the report. The column headings have been added to the printout to show what each column contains but they are not quite the same as the field names – for instance 'Total owed' is a summary of the data in all of the records. The actual total is calculated by the computer. It adds all the **BALANCE** values for the selected records and puts the answer in the space reserved for it in the report. Most database programs can add up the values in the same field in each record and can do other calculations such as finding the average of all values.

Customers Owing Money

Customer number	Title	Initials	Surname	Account Bal.
0001	Mr	P.	Smith	-£233.56
0002	Mrs	S.	Ahmed	-£125.73
0003	Ms	P.J.	Wells	-£599.36
0005	Ms	D.	Lawrence	-£45.50
0006	Mr	L.	Bedford	-£800.00
0007	Mrs	K.A.	Wilson	-£523.21
0009	Mr	K.S.	Dhillon	-£2.30
0010	Mrs	V.N.	Patel	-£264.21
0016	Mr	J.	Graham	-£71.23
0018	Mr	T.	Bates	-£523.00
0019	Miss	T.	Piejus	-£350.00
0020	Mr	A	McFall	-£605.85
0021	Mr	J.H.	Penny	-£695.20
0023	Mrs	J.G.	Smith	-£42.00
0025	Ms	I.D.	Gallagher	-£32.00
			Total Owed	-£4,913.15

Figure 2.3 Part of the database file showing which customers still owe money.

This is for information which will only appear at the top of the printed report pages.

This is where the information for each selected record appears.

This is for the summary information and it will appear only at the end of the printed report.

Figure 2.4 The areas that make up a database report.

SETTING UP A REPORT

A report like this has to be set up using the report designer in the database package before it can be used. Each database package does this differently, but most of them divide the report into at least three areas, as you can see in Figure 2.4.

Your database package might give you an extra area to put in the title of the report, and also for page summaries as well as the final report summary. When you set up the report any fixed information, like headings or explanations, is put into the places where it must appear. The fields that will appear for each record are **selected** and placed in the correct places in the **record area**. This only needs to be done for one record – the database package will work out how many records it can fit on a page when it prints the report and will set out each record in the same way.

When the layout for the report has been set up you can save it on disk as a report format with its own name. (The name you give it should tell you something about what the report is for.) The system might have limits on the length of the name, and might not allow spaces so you might have to call the monthly report 'Month' and the customer list just 'Customer'.

To get the printout shown in Figure 2.3, we need to do two things:

1 Select the records needed by searching for **BALANCE < 0**
2 Print the selected records using the correct report format.

Reports are not always lists. A report can be set up to print letters containing data from the records. For example, when customers don't pay their bills on time Ms Stillwell sends a reminder slip, in the format shown in Figure 2.5. She then prints them onto headed paper and sends them out to each customer who has owed money for more than 28 days.

When Ms Stillwell sets up this report format, all the fixed information and the field contents go into the record area so that everything is printed out for each record, and a page break is inserted at the bottom of the record so that each record is printed on a new sheet of paper.

The search used to select the records for this report is:

BALANCE < 0 AND LAST __ ORDER < 01.08.93.

When she has selected the records, Ms Stillwell chooses the 'Reminder' report format – and the reminders are printed.

Q

What do we mean by a report?

Describe two different ways in which a report can be laid out.

Design a layout for a different report which might be useful to Ms Stillwell. What search command is needed for this report?

REMINDER OF PAYMENT DUE

Customer Number	0001
Name	Mr P Smith
Date of last order	27.04.94
Current balance of account	-£233.56

Our terms are payment within 28 days.
Payment is now outstanding

PAYMENT IS REQUESTED WITHIN SEVEN DAYS

Figure 2.5 *The format used for a reminder slip, prepared from the database described in this chapter.*

Summary

- A database is a store of data which the computer can read. It can be accessed in many different ways.
- A file is a collection of related records.
- A record contains information about one person or thing. It is divided into fields.
- A field contains only one piece of data.
- Data is extracted by searching the database.
- Searches can be based on a unique value in one field to find a single record.

- Searches can find groups of records with a particular value in one field.

- More complex searches can be carried out by looking for specific values in more than one field.

- The output from a database is called a report.

- Lots of different reports can be produced from a single database.

SKILLS

When you have completed the work in this chapter you should be able to:

- Search an existing database to find one record.

- Search for groups of records with one or more things in common.

- Select and print out the report you want.

Questions

I Explain what each of the following terms means:

File
Record
Field
Database

2 Why is it important that the data we put into a database is accurate?

Creating Your Own Database

W hen you create any kind of computer system, the process is divided up into these main stages:

▶ Identifying a need.

▶ Analysing what you must do to meet that need.

▶ Designing what you are going to produce.

▶ Implementing and testing your design.

▶ Evaluating how well your design meets the need.

The first step in creating your own database is to identify a need for a store of data which can be retrieved, perhaps in several different ways. The database you decide to set up yourself may be for use in one of the subjects you are studying at school or it may be concerned with an activity outside school. (You will find a list of suggested topics at the end of this chapter.)

A database is useful when:

▶ There is a large amount of information to be stored.

▶ The information fits into a regular pattern so each record can have the same structure.

▶ The database you set up will be used for more than one purpose or will be used more than once.

Once you have identified a need for a database you need to decide what the database must be able to produce. To do this you will need to think about the purpose of the database, the people who will use it and what they will want to know. When you have a clear idea of what you want your database to achieve you can begin the design work. Start by making a list of all the reports you need, with a description of what each one will contain. A very simple database system may only need one kind of report, but most will need two or more.

In the example in this chapter we will see how we can design and set up a database. Our database is to be used by the secretary of a fan club, who is the **end-user**. We must remember that we have to meet all the requirements of this end-user if our database system is to be a success.

Stage 1: Identifying a need

The fan club we are working for has an expanding membership and the secretary is finding it difficult to keep in touch with everyone. A membership database will make the secretary's job much easier. Using a database is sensible because:

1   There are lots of members in the fan club (there is a lot of data).
2   We will have to store the same facts about each person so the data about each member will easily fit into the same pattern.
3   The secretary writes to the members regularly about different things so the data will be used many times and in different ways

Stage 2: Analysing what's needed

During this stage we look at what the club secretary wants the database system to do and identify the outputs we need.

1   The club has to send out material (such as newsletters) to all its members so the database must be able to produce name and address labels. These will have the member's name on one line and the address divided up into four lines, including the postcode.
2   Members sometimes forget to renew their subscriptions so the database must be able to produce letters to remind them that their subscription is due. These letters will need to be posted so name and address labels will be required as well.
3   Sometimes the club has special offers. The secretary thinks it might be useful to print a list of the members who have bought special offers in the past. This list should contain the member's number, name, address and a code number for the last offer purchased.

> **Q**
>
> Write down the main stages in the creation of any computer system.
>
> It is important to know when a database would be useful. Describe three situations where you think a database would be useful.

Stage 3: Designing what is to be produced

This stage is divided up into steps as there is quite a lot of designing to do.

STEP 1: IDENTIFYING THE INPUTS NEEDED

We have to work out what has to be stored in the database to produce the outputs we need.

1 The club needs to store names and addresses. The address will need to be split up so that labels can be printed.
2 Each member should have a unique membership number so there is no chance of mixing up members with the same name. The date when the subscription was paid will have to be stored to produce the reminders.
3 The code number of the last offer purchased will have to be stored to produce the required list.

STEP 2: CHOOSING THE RECORD STRUCTURE

We must now decide on the record structure. We have to work out how many fields we will have in each record and what should go into each field.

These fields have to be given names. Database packages don't always allow spaces in field names, so if we want to include a space we may have to put something in it. The best character to use is the underline character (_). If we want a field called LAST OFFER we could call it LAST_OFFER. Often the length of a field name is limited as well, so we should give our fields fairly short names.

We have to decide how big each field needs to be to fit in all the characters needed (the **field length**). Fields can be of different types as well. A **field type** controls the kind of data which can be stored in the field.

▶ Character (or text) fields hold words and other characters (like @ or &).

▶ Numeric fields hold numbers, and you can usually fix the number of decimal places allowed. Some packages allow you to specify the **range** of numbers allowed.

▶ Date fields hold dates, using two numbers for each of day, month and year. The date 25 May 1997 would be entered as 25/05/97 in a date field. The order is described as DDMMYY.

▶ Another field type is the logical or true/false field. This can hold a single letter or number to indicate whether the value in the record is true or false.

You can see the record structure we need for the fan club database file in Figure 3.1.

Not all database programs need you to specify the field length and field type when you set up the record structure. Some don't have a field type called 'date'. If this type isn't available in your database package you should store the date in a numeric field in the order YYMMDD to make comparisons easy. For example, you should store the date 25 May 1997 as 970525.

Field Name	Length	Type
Membership_no.	5	Numeric
Member_name	25	Alphanumeric
Address_1	30	Alphanumeric
Address_2	30	Alphanumeric
Address_3	30	Alphanumeric
Postcode	7	Alphanumeric
Subscription_date	8	Date
Last_offer	2	Numeric

Figure 3.1 *The record structure for a fan club's database.*

When you are deciding field lengths, think of the longest possible input for this field and use that length. For example, you will probably always need a longer field for the first line of the address than for the line containing the postcode.

STEP 3: IDENTIFYING THE PROCESSING NEEDED

We must decide what searches the database program will have to do to select the correct records to produce the reports. This is the processing needed to get the reports the club secretary wants.

1   To produce the name and address labels no searching is needed – a label will be printed for each member. The order these labels are printed in doesn't matter so there is no need to get the database file into a particular order before printing.

2   For the subscription reminder notices the secretary needs to select those records with a SUBSCRIPTION_DATE of more than 1 year ago. The search to be used will be:

$$SUBSCRIPTION\_DATE < TARGET \ DATE.$$

The target date is the earliest date when the subscription is still valid. For example:

$$SUBSCRIPTION\_DATE < 01.06.93$$

The records found are printed using the 'reminder notice' report format and then printed again using the 'label' report format to produce a set of address labels.

3   The special offers list must include the records which contain a number greater than zero in the LAST_OFFER field, meaning the member did buy something in the last special offer. The date search used will be

$$LAST\_OFFER > 0$$

The records found will be printed using the 'offer list' report.

STEP 4: DESIGNING THE REPORTS

Each of the printouts needed has to be designed carefully so that it contains all the necessary information, the layout will be clear and everything will fit properly. Remember, you will often need to add headings or explanations, as well as the field contents, so the reader knows exactly what all the information means.

Always work out your design on squared paper first. This helps you fit everything in and gives you an idea of how the report will look. Take care to put each item in the correct area of the report. Our design for the label report is shown in Figure 3.2, and for the offers list in Figure 3.3.

Q

Describe the details needed to create a record structure.

Why should database programs without a 'date' field type store dates in the form YYMMDD?

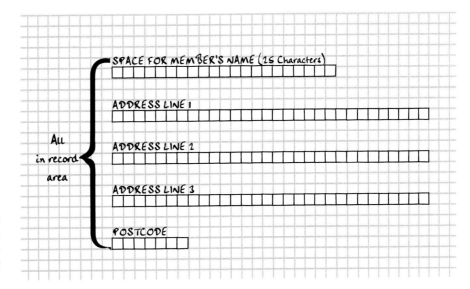

Figure 3.2 *The design for the label report for our fan club database. You can see that the address lines need to be longer than the one for the post code.*

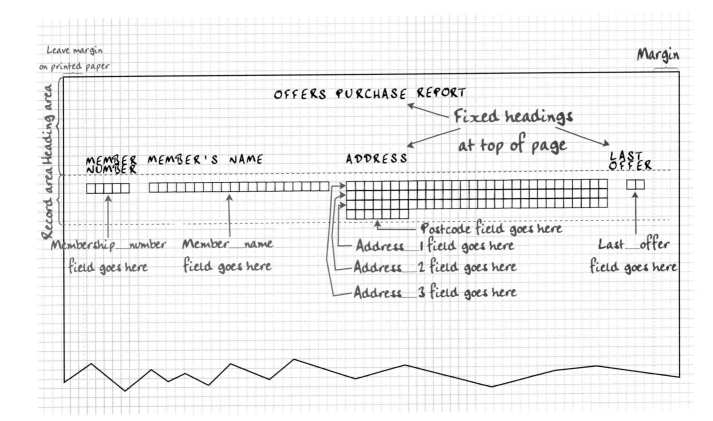

Figure 3.3 *The design for the offers report. This report needs the area for headings, which the label report didn't.*

We can set up the subscription reminder as a database report or we can type the reminder letter using a word processor and take the member's name and subscription date from the database record and put it into the correct place in the letter. This is called **mail merging**.

If we choose to use a database report we can design it on squared paper, with all of the text of the letter in the record area (you can see an example in Figure 3.4).

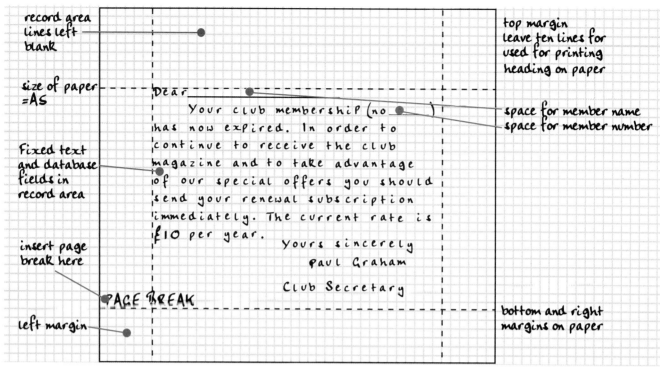

Figure 3.4 The design for the subscription reminder, produced as a database report.

If we decide to produce the letters using mail merging then we will type the letter out using a word processor package capable of **importing** data from the database. We mark the places where data is to be put in and specify the file name and field names to be used. The way we do this will depend on the package used. The layout diagram in Figure 3.5 shows where data from the database will be inserted.

Figure 3.5 Mail merging - how data from a database is inserted into a standard letter.

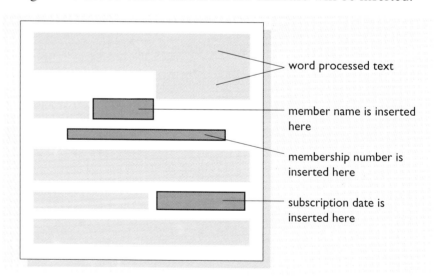

- word processed text
- member name is inserted here
- membership number is inserted here
- subscription date is inserted here

STEP 5: DESIGNING THE DATA COLLECTION SHEET

A data collection sheet is a form that people fill in and which is used as the source of the data which goes into the database. For example, when a new member joins the fan club she will fill in all her details on a data collection form (this is sometimes called a data capture form).

When we design the form we must make sure that the person filling it in will write down the information they are supplying in the way we want it. We should always try to keep the order logical. People expect to give their name and address together when they fill in the form so we shouldn't ask for them to put their name at the top and their address somewhere at the bottom. If we expect a particular length of response then we should indicate on the form the number of spaces that are available, otherwise people will write things that don't fit into the database fields. The person filling in the form must be given very clear instructions so they're not left guessing about what they should write. Don't collect information you don't need. The design for the data collection form for the fan club is shown in Figure 3.6.

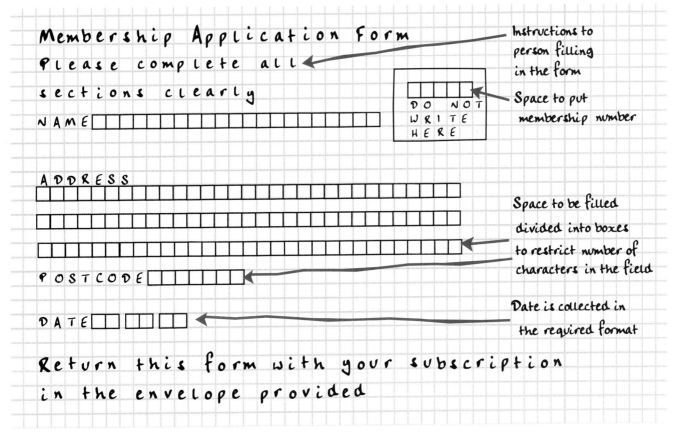

Figure 3.6 *Design for the data collection form.*

■ *Stage 4: Implementing and testing the design*

This stage is also quite complex, so it has also been broken down into steps.

STEP 1: SETTING UP THE DATABASE STRUCTURE AND THE REPORTS

With the database software package loaded into the computer, we create a new file for the fan club database. We name the fields in the record and enter any necessary information about field length and field type. It should then be saved to disk. When you want to enter data into your database you might find that the fields are displayed in the order you have put them in the record. Some database packages allow you to set up special input forms. Whichever method you use, you must make sure the data is entered in the same order as it appears on the data collection sheet. If your database package displays the field names in order for data entry, then the order of the fields in the record must be the same as the order the data is collected.

Next we use the report design part of the database package to set up each report, working from the design sheets. We give these reports names or numbers and save them on disk.

We produce data collection sheets, using a suitable word processor package. (Chapter 4 covers word processing.)

STEP 2: PUTTING DATA INTO THE DATABASE FOR TESTING

Now we enter some of the data so that we can test the database system. We don't have to put in all the data at this stage but we must enter enough for all the tests we need. We must be careful that the data we choose will test all the parts of the database system. At the very least we need:

▶ A record for a member who paid their subscription within the last year so we can check that we don't send reminders to people who have paid.

▶ A record for a member who didn't pay their subscription when it was due, so we can check that we do produce a reminder when one is needed.

▶ A record for a member who has bought a special offer, to check that this person appears on the offers list.

▶ A record for a member who has never bought a special offer, to check that this person does not appear on the offers list.

▶ It is a good idea to include an incomplete record as well, to see what happens if some of the field entries are missing.

We need to be very careful in working out the test data to be sure that all the searches will find records that contain the required data and leave out records which don't contain the required data.

You can see the data that must be entered for testing purposes in Figure 3.7.

00065	Mr M Evans	14 Warwick Road Buxey Marway	M27 5BW	12.11.94	7
00052	Ms L. Black	83 Bailey Towers Bolton Road Rightmead	R56 1BD	18.08.94	0
00345	Mr G. Sing	28 High Street Foxley	F8 5TF	05.06.93	3
00012	Ms A. Moru	8 Coppel Place Shipdale	S18 6DD	05.06.93	5
00078	Mr G. Nevin	55 Barron Way Gawley	G15 4LB		

Figure 3.7 *Data to be used for testing the database.*

STEP 3: CARRYING OUT THE TESTS

1 **Testing printing of labels**

We select the labels report and give a print instruction. This should print out the address labels. The printout must be checked to make sure that it matches the design and that the data printed out is from the correct fields – it is also important to check that it fits the labels!

2 **Testing printing of subscription reminders**

To check that subscription reminder letters are produced properly we have to carry out a search (searches are often referred to as queries). Many packages have no way of saving a search or query, so you'd have to enter it each time you search. The search we need to use is

SUBSCRIPTION_DATE < 01.01.94

This will select the records for members whose subscriptions are overdue. We then choose the reminder report from the list of reports available and print out the letters. We must check the letters to make sure that the correct records have been selected. We must check the layout of the letter to make sure that the fields are appearing in the right places and that everything fits on the page. When the letters are done we print out the labels for these selected records.

3   Testing printing of the last offers list

To make sure the last offers list prints correctly we must do a different search. This time the search we need is

LAST_OFFER > 0

This will select all the records where an offer number has been entered. To get the list printed out we choose the 'offer list' report from the list of available reports and give a print instruction. Again, we must check that the printed output is laid out as we expect and that the correct records and fields have been inserted.

STEP 4: WRITING INSTRUCTIONS

The secretary of the fan club will need some instructions so that he can use the database. These instructions (often called the **user guide**) must be very clear and must cover all the things the user might reasonably expect to be able to do with the database. In this case we should explain how to print out each of the reports. We also need to explain how to add, edit and delete records so that he can keep the data up to date. User instructions should also explain how to make **backup copies** of the database, what to do if something goes wrong and how to get back data which has been lost by using the latest backup copy.

When we write these instructions we must be careful about the use of technical terms. The fan club secretary might not be very familiar with computers and databases so we need to explain words which might not be understood.

Q

What would you expect to find in the user instructions for a database?

Remember - any database which contains personal information about living people has to be registered under the Data Protection Act unless it is exempt. Our fan club database would have to be registered unless all the members had agreed to the data being stored on computer.

■ *Stage 5: Evaluating the database system*

I t is always important to look at what has been achieved. We need to be sure that the database we have set up is doing everything the fan club secretary wants. We can also look for ways to improve the database system.

Summary

The stages involved in setting up your own database are:

- **Identify a need**. It doesn't make sense to set up a big database to carry out a single search. If there isn't very much data it is usually better to deal with it manually.

- **Analyse**. Work out what the database should be capable of producing.

- **Design**. Work out what will have to be stored to produce the required outputs. Decide what processing will be needed. Decide on the record structure. Design the reports and data capture sheets.

- **Implement**. Set up the database record structure and reports. Produce data collection forms.

- **Test**. Make sure the system works as it should.

- **Document**. Write instructions for the person using the database.

- **Evaluate**. Look at what has been done and check if the system meets the requirements. See if it could be improved.

Suggested topics for database work

Here are a few ideas for databases you could set up yourself. They have been divided up into different subject areas.

GEOGRAPHY

A database about the use of buildings in your area could produce reports on uses of buildings in particular streets and locations of all the buildings used for a particular purpose.

A database about local tourist attractions could provide lists of attractions of different types with information on opening hours and transport details.

HISTORY

A database about local historical figures could be used to produce lists of people with certain achievements – for example a list of local people involved in the foundation of charities.

SCIENCE

A database about animals and plants in the school grounds could be used to produce reports on animals in a particular habitat (such as a pond), animals of a particular type and animals and plants seen at a particular time of year.

A database about chemicals could provide reports on chemicals important in particular industries, chemicals which are harmful pollutants, and chemicals with particular properties.

TECHNOLOGY/DESIGN AND TECHNOLOGY

A database about materials could be used to produce reports on materials with certain properties, materials within a specified price range or materials available in specified sizes.

NON-SCHOOL RELATED DATABASES

If you don't want to work on a database related to a school subject then you could try one of these.

A *zoo database*, to produce reports on different animals, animals from different continents and animals in danger of extinction.

A *library database*, to produce reports on overdue books, books on various subjects and books which are on loan.

SKILLS

After completing the work in this chapter you should be able to:

- Examine a task and decide if it makes sense to use a computer database to handle the information.

- For any particular task, decide what reports the database has to produce and what must be in these reports.

- Design record structures which let you store all the data you will need to create the reports.

- Produce detailed report designs.

- Work from these designs to set up a database.

- Design and produce data collection sheets.

- Select test data and test that a database system works correctly.

- Write good, clear user instructions.

- Evaluate a database system, decide if it meets the requirements of the end user and suggest how it could be improved.

Questions

1 A school uses a computer system to help with administration. The computer has a database which stores data about the teachers, pupils and rooms.

  a Describe three different ways of presenting the output from the database.
  b A new pupil joins the school. How could the computer system be used to help fit the pupil into suitable classes?

MEG sample material

2 Pupils are constructing a database of chemical elements. The fields they use are:

  element
  atomic number
  symbol
  melting point
  boiling point

MEG sample material

Describe a suitable structure for the database.

3 Describe how you would create an information-handling system to process the results of a sports day. Give reasons for your choices.

MEG sample material

4 A company uses a computer to put buyers of second-hand cars in touch with people who are selling cars. It collects information from sellers by getting them to complete a form. Buyers can then telephone the company and ask for a list of people who have the sort of car they want.

  a What type of software would be most suitable?
  b Design a form for inputting the information from a seller.

SEG specimen paper

5 A geography database is to be used to produce several reports on tourist attractions. One will be used to list places with beaches, another will list places of historical interest. Each list will name three hotels in each town and two main attractions, and will give the name of the nearest airport.

  a Identify the data items that will have to be stored to produce each report.
  b Work out the fields you will need in each record in the database.
  c Design the report layouts.

6 Why is data sometimes coded when it is entered into a computer?

7 How is data stored in a database easier to handle than information stored in a filing cabinet?

8 Describe, in order, the steps you would take to design and set up a database.

9 A video club hires out films to its members. The club uses separate database files to store details about:

films
members
film hiring.

The table below shows part of the films database file.

FILM NUMBER	FILM NAME	FILM CATEGORY	RATING	HIRE CHARGE
0123	Mermaids	Comedy	15	£2.00
0124	JFK	Drama	15	£2.50
0254	Star wars	Adventure	U	£1.50
0361	Mad Max 2	Adventure	18	£2.00
0422	City Slickers	Comedy	15	£125
0774	Die Hard 2	Adventure	18	£1.50
0813	Blackadder	Comady	15	£1.50

a If you look at the information in the table about the film Blackadder you will see a typing mistake – Comady should be Comedy.

(i) Which three of the following steps would you use in order to correct the mistake?

A   Print the whole database
B   Save the changes
C   Correct the mistake
D   Delete the whole database
E   Select the Blackadder record

(ii) Look at the information in the table again. Which other piece of information is probably a mistake?

b From the list below, choose items of information that would be suitable for the FILMS_HIRED database file.

Address of the club   Film name   Member's name
Original cost of film   Date of birth   Film number
Name of club manager   Membership number   Film category
Hire date   Phone number   Length of hire

c Describe two lists that could be produced to help the club manager which would be easier to obtain using the FILMS database rather than simply by storing paper records. Explain why each list would be useful.

d Write down the instructions or steps you might use if you wanted the FILMS database to display a list of Adventure films which are rated 18 and cost less than £2.00 to hire.

Questions cont'd

e From the list below, choose items of information that would be suitable for the MEMBERS database file.

Address of the club   Film name   Member's name
Original cost of film   Date of birth   Film number
Name of club manager   Membership number   Film category
Hire date   Phone number   Length of hire

f When new members join the video club they fill in an application form. This form is used to enter information into the MEMBERS database file. Design a form that would be suitable for this.

NEAB specimen material

10 A database contains census data from a small village in 1841. The database contains text from original documents of the time.

a Give two reasons why it is an advantage to have all the data stored as a database.

MEG sample material

b Why might historians criticise the use of the database?

11 Schools keep information about their pupils on a large database. This list shows some of the information about a few pupils in one school.

SURNAME	FORENAME	SEX	DATE OF BIRTH
Pabla	Davinder	M	4.11.76
Pace	Lucy	F	30.6.78
Pacey	Lauren	F	11.3.77
Packer	Keith	M	17.3.78
Padgett	John	M	1.5.77
Page	Helena	F	25.9.76
Painter	Samuel	M	28.6.79
Pailing	Robert	M	22.11.76
Palmer	Janina	F	6.9.77

Explain how you could search the database to produce a list of the girls in year 11 (Born between 1 September 1976 and 31 August 1977).

MEG sample material

4 Communicating Information – Word Processing

■ IT and communication

Information technology (IT) has had a huge impact on the way information is provided. One of the most obvious uses of IT is in preparing written information using **word processors** and **desktop publishing (DTP)** packages, but we also use IT to prepare and communicate visual information (pictures and graphs), using art and **graphics** packages. Film makers use computer generated images and animation to make animated (cartoon) films and also in combination with film using real actors. The animated film *An American Tail* was made using computer generated images including moving background images and in *Who Framed Roger Rabbit?* many sequences were produced by combining animation, computer images and real people.

Computers can be used to generate background images for cartoon films such as An American Tail.

Human action can also be combined with computer animation to produce realistic effects as in Who Framed Roger Rabbit?

IT is also vital in producing music and sound effects. Using computers we can sample, store, retrieve, mix, edit and distort sounds in various ways. The resulting sounds could not be produced by any conventional musical instruments (see Chapter 7 for more about sound).

Write down three ways of using IT to communicate information.

Try to find out what is meant by the technique of 'morphing' which is used in film production.

Computers are used in sound recording to mix different sounds.

Multimedia presentations use a combination of high resolution pictures, video sequences, sound and text to present information. Multimedia presentation requires huge amounts of stored data – **CD-ROM** is often used to store it instead of magnetic disks.

In the rest of this chapter we will look at word processing. You will find out more about graphics in Chapter 6 and about sound in Chapter 7.

Word processing

You are most likely to begin to use IT to communicate information using a word processor to produce a piece of written work – perhaps a review of a film you've seen.

ADVANTAGES OF WORD PROCESSORS

Using a word processing package to prepare and print text has several advantages over using pen and paper or an old fashioned typewriter:

▶ Altering what you have typed (either to correct mistakes or to improve and rearrange your first draft) is easy.

▶ You can save your document on disk and reload it any time you need it.

▶ You can save standard layouts for documents, so if you want to produce lots of similar documents you can put them together more quickly than if you had to start from the beginning each time.

▶ Many word processor packages allow you to bring in (import) material from other packages (like pictures, charts and data from databases) so you can produce impressive reports easily and quickly.

▮ *Using a word processor*

The things you can do with a word processor will depend on the package you are using, but all packages will at least allow you to do the following:

▶ Insert text

▶ Delete text

▶ Justify text

▶ Move text around

▶ Alter the margins

▶ Alter the line spacing

▶ Use tabs

▶ Alter the way the text looks (for example by using underlining, italic, bold or changing the font).

When you begin to use a word processor or start to use a new word processing program it is a good idea to use an existing **text file** to find out how to carry out basic editing tasks. Most word processing packages have a few of these text files for you to experiment with and to practice your word processing skills. Once you are familiar with the operations your word processor offers you will be able to produce tidy, impressive documents in whatever style you choose.

Let's look at a few of these features in more detail.

DELETING TEXT

To **delete text** (or 'rub it out') you move the **cursor** (a line or block which shows where you are in the document) to the end of the text you want to delete and press the backspace or delete key to remove the unwanted material. When you delete something the package rearranges the remaining text to fill up the space, as it has done in Figure 4.1.

Rabbits

Rabbits are small mammals. They live as wild animals but tame ones are often kept as pets. (Wild rabbits are a grey-brown colour.) Tame rabbits come in a variety of different colours. They can also be more than one colour. Some are white with black ears, paws and noses.

Rabbits

Rabbits are small mammals. They live as wild animals but tame ones are often kept as pets. Tame rabbits come in a variety of different colours. They can also be more than one colour. Some are white with black ears, paws and noses.

Figure 4.1 *Deleting text. The sentence circled in the top sample of text has been deleted from the one at the bottom. Note that the rest of the paragraph has been rearranged to close up the gap.*

INSERTING TEXT

To **insert** or add text, move the cursor to the position where you want the new words to go. Make sure that your word processor will make room for the extra text, rather than typing over what is already there and then type in the extra text. The package moves the rest of the text to make a space for what you have typed in. Figure 4.2 shows how text has been reshuffled to fit in inserted text.

Rabbits
Rabbits are small mammals. They live as wild animals but tame ones are often kept as pets. Tame rabbits come in a variety of different colours. They can also be more than one colour. Some are white with black ears, paws and noses.

Rabbits
Rabbits are small mammals. They live as wild animals but tame ones are often kept as pets. Rabbits eat corn and cereals, hay and green foods such as grass, lettuce and cabbage. Tame rabbits come in a variety of different colours. They can also be more than one colour. Some are white with black ears, paws and noses.

Figure 4.2 *Inserting text. An extra sentence (circled) has been inserted in the text at the bottom. The rest of the paragraph has automatically been rearranged to make room for the new material.*

CHANGING THE MARGINS

If you alter the **margins** of your document the package rearranges the text to fit it in (you can see this in Figure 4.3). In some older word processing packages you will have to alter each paragraph separately.

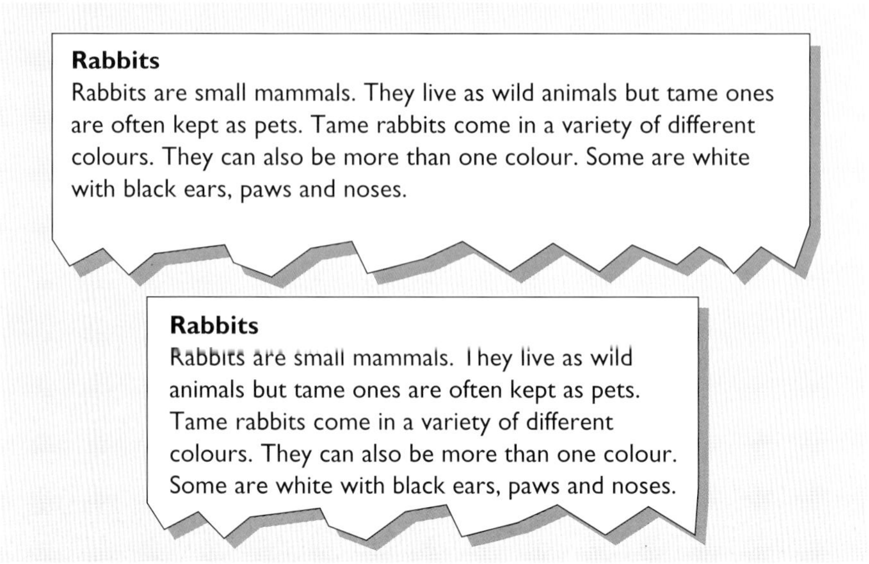

Rabbits
Rabbits are small mammals. They live as wild animals but tame ones are often kept as pets. Tame rabbits come in a variety of different colours. They can also be more than one colour. Some are white with black ears, paws and noses.

Rabbits
Rabbits are small mammals. They live as wild animals but tame ones are often kept as pets. Tame rabbits come in a variety of different colours. They can also be more than one colour. Some are white with black ears, paws and noses.

Figure 4.3   Changing the margins of a block of text. The margins in the top sample have been changed to give the sample at the bottom. All the text has been rearranged to fit the new margins.

UNDERLINING TEXT

Underlining is often used to distinguish headings (as in Figure 4.4) or to emphasise important words (other ways of doing this are to use

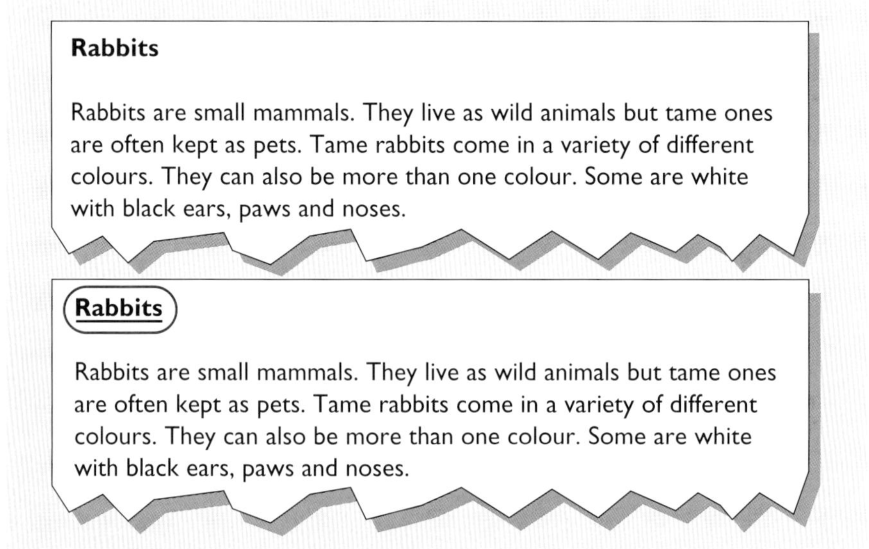

Rabbits

Rabbits are small mammals. They live as wild animals but tame ones are often kept as pets. Tame rabbits come in a variety of different colours. They can also be more than one colour. Some are white with black ears, paws and noses.

Rabbits

Rabbits are small mammals. They live as wild animals but tame ones are often kept as pets. Tame rabbits come in a variety of different colours. They can also be more than one colour. Some are white with black ears, paws and noses.

Figure 4.4   The heading in the sample at the bottom has been underlined to make it more noticeable.

italic or **bold** text). To underline text, turn on the underlining option at the start of the text to be underlined and turn it off at the end. If you have already typed the words you might need to move the cursor and put special markers at each end of the text you want underlined or you may have to highlight the text by moving the cursor across it then select the underline option.

WORKING WITH BLOCKS OF TEXT

You can handle **blocks of text** all at once. Different packages use different methods of marking the block of text you want to do something with – you might have to move the cursor to the start and add a special 'start of block' marker then move the cursor to the end and add an 'end of block marker. In other packages you can **select** the text by highlighting it using the mouse. Once you have marked the block you can move it, copy it or delete it. Figure 4.5 shows how a block of text has been moved.

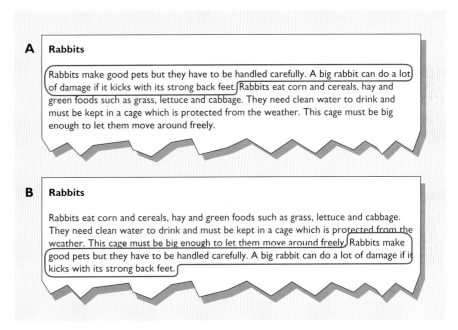

A Rabbits

Rabbits make good pets but they have to be handled carefully. A big rabbit can do a lot of damage if it kicks with its strong back feet. Rabbits eat corn and cereals, hay and green foods such as grass, lettuce and cabbage. They need clean water to drink and must be kept in a cage which is protected from the weather. This cage must be big enough to let them move around freely.

B Rabbits

Rabbits eat corn and cereals, hay and green foods such as grass, lettuce and cabbage. They need clean water to drink and must be kept in a cage which is protected from the weather. This cage must be big enough to let them move around freely. Rabbits make good pets but they have to be handled carefully. A big rabbit can do a lot of damage if it kicks with its strong back feet.

Figure 4.5 *Moving blocks of text. The sentence circled in the text at the top has been moved to a new position.*

ALTERING LINE SPACING

You can alter the space between lines of text. The spacing you can use is probably either **single spacing**, with the lines close together (this book is printed single spaced) or **double spacing**, with more space between each line of text (you can see an example in Figure 4.6). Some packages allow you to vary the **line spacing** more. You can set line spacing for the whole of your document when you begin or can alter it as you go along. Use the line space command where you want the change to happen.

> **Rabbits**
>
> Rabbits make good pets but they have to be handled carefully. A big rabbit can do a lot
>
> of damage if it kicks with its strong back feet. Rabbits eat corn and cereals, hay and
>
> green foods such as grass, lettuce and cabbage. They need clean water to drink and
>
> must be kept in a cage which is protected from the weather. This cage must be big
>
> enough to let them move around freely.

Figure 4.6 *Here is some text that is double spaced - the space between the lines is very large.*

JUSTIFYING TEXT

The **justification** of the text is the way it is arranged on each line. You can choose to have your text **fully justified**, which means that the spacing between the words is adjusted so that they fill the whole line and the right and left edges are both even (as in Figure 4.7).

> **Rabbits**
>
> Rabbits make good pets but they have to be handled carefully. A big rabbit can do a lot
> of damage if it kicks with its strong back feet. Rabbits eat corn and cereals, hay and
> green foods such as grass, lettuce and cabbage. They need clean water to drink and
> must be kept in a cage which is protected from the weather. This cage must be big
> enough to let them move around freely.

Figure 4.7 *This text has been set fully justified - both edges of the text are straight.*

You can also have text left or right justified. When you **left justify** your text the package arranges it so that it lines up along the left hand side of the page, and the right hand side is uneven. If you **right justify** your text it all lines up along the right hand side of the page, but the left side is uneven (examples in Figure 4.8).

> **Rabbits**
>
> Rabbits make good pets but they have to be handled carefully. A big rabbit can do a lot
> of damage if it kicks with its strong back feet. Rabbits eat corn and cereals, hay and
> green foods such as grass, lettuce and cabbages. They need clean water to drink and
> must be kept in a cage which is protected from the weather. This cage must be big
> enough to let them move around freely.

Figure 4.8 *A piece of text that has been set left justified. You can see that the left hand edge is even, but the right hand edge is jagged.*

You can also **centre** your text. The package will arrange what you type so that it is in a central position between the margins. You will find centred text useful for headings and titles and can see an example in Figure 4.9.

Rabbits

Rabbits make good pets but they have to be handled carefully. A big rabbit can do a lot of damage if it kicks with its strong back feet. Rabbits eat corn and cereals, hay and green foods such as grass, lettuce and cabbages. They need clean water to drink and must be kept in a cage which is protected from the weather. This cage must be big enough to let them move around freely.

Figure 4.9 *The heading has been centred over the text in this example. Note that the text is still fully justified.*

USING TABS

Tabs are a way of moving the text cursor in bigger steps than the space bar. They are very useful for typing tables as you can use them to make sure all your columns line up. Your package probably has some tab markers already set, but if these are not what you want you can set your own. You will need to find out how this is done on the package you are using.

OTHER FEATURES

Your word processor may have other features, including different fonts in different sizes, like those in Figure 4.10. Find out what extra features your package provides and learn how to use them.

Figure 4.10 *Some of the huge number of fonts you can use in word processing.*

SAVING AND PRINTING

When you are sure you understand those editing commands and can carry them out, try **saving** and **printing** your work.

Be sensible - always use your word processor's features sensibly – too many different fonts and sizes on one page will look untidy and disorganised and the impact of the page will be lost. When you are producing word processed text you should think about the people who will read it and what information you are trying to get across.

Questions

Find out the name of the word processing package you use in school. Write down the commands needed or the methods used to:

- delete text
- insert text
- underline text
- change the margins
- change the justification
- change the line spacing
- set a tab stop
- move a block of text

Describe one way in which you have made use of word processing in school.

Summary

- Information can be communicated in several different ways.
- When you use a word processor you can correct mistakes easily.
- A word processor lets you rearrange your work.
- You can save your work on disk and load it again later to make more copies or to edit your document.

SKILLS

After completing the work in this chapter you should be able to:

- Produce a neat and tidy piece of work, using your word processing package to control the position of the text on the page.
- Save your work, reload it and print it.
- Use the editing facilities in your word processing package to alter and reorganise your work.
- Use different styles of text, underlining and different fonts to add impact to what you write.

Questions

1 In the table below, tick two items that are advantages that a word processor has over a typewriter.

The ribbon is changed automatically
It is quicker because the carriage returns automatically
It uses less paper
Work can be checked on screen before printing
The keyboard is smaller
The print is clearer

MEG sample material

2 Your Food Technology teacher has used a word processor to type out a recipe for a Victoria Sandwich cake.

---

1 Grease and line two sandwich tins. Heat the oven to 170° (mark 4).

2 Fold in the sifted flour and baking powder. Divide the mixture beteen the two tin and bake the cakes for about 25 minutes.

3 Cream together the margarine and sgar. Beat in the eggs one at a time.

4 Leave to cool and layer the cake with strawberry jam.

However, she has made two typing errors and has copied out the recipe in the wrong order. Explain how you could use IT to detect and correct the errors and the order of the paragraphs without retyping the whole recipe.

MEG sample material

5

Communicating information – Graphics

Graphics is a general term that is used to describe all the different kinds of pictures, drawings, charts and graphs that can be produced using a computer.

Graphics can be produced on a computer using **drawing packages, painting packages, computer aided design (CAD) packages** or **charting packages**. Some word processors allow you to produce graphics and many spreadsheets can be used to produce graphs and charts.

Choosing a graphics package

Before you choose a particular graphics package you must think about what you want to produce.

▶ If you need to produce accurate graphs and charts working from data you have collected then the graphics facilities of a spreadsheet package or a charting package will give the best results.

▶ If you need to illustrate a report or produce a poster then a drawing or a painting package will be best.

▶ CAD packages are good for accurately drawing to scale – for example when drawing designs for buildings or electronic circuits.

Let's look at the various packages in more detail.

Painting packages

U sing a painting package you can 'paint' on the screen. Even simple packages let you do the following:

- Draw lines and shapes using the mouse.
- Use various ready-made shapes such as circles and rectangles.
- **Fill** in your shapes with different colours and patterns.
- 'Rub out' mistakes using the eraser tool.
- Spray colours on the screen using a spray tool.
- **Zoom** in on parts of the picture to alter small details.
- Print your picture out.
- Save your picture on disk so you can reuse it or change it later.

The picture in Figure 5.1 was made using a painting package. The first parts drawn were the sky and the sea. These are rectangles filled with colour. Everything else was drawn on top of this background. The birds started as lines and were altered slightly by zooming in on them and changing the colour of a few spots (each spot on the screen is called a **pixel**). The clouds were built up by spraying white and grey onto the sky. The cliff was painted using the mouse, in green and brown. It was then tidied up and the white foam was added by zooming in and altering the colour of some of the pixels. The boat was painted and tidied up in the same way.

Painting packages are usually very easy to learn to use but don't have as many facilities as drawing packages. The pictures are saved on disk by storing data about the colour of each spot on the screen. You can't usually change the size of parts of the picture and if you try to alter the size of the whole picture you could be disappointed with the result.

Figure 5.1 *A graphic drawn using a painting package.*

Drawing packages

Drawing programs have lots of different tools to make it easy to produce pictures. Using a drawing package you can:

▶ use straight lines or draw freehand lines as needed

▶ use ready-made shapes, such as circles and rectangles, which you can place anywhere in your drawing. You can adjust the size of these shapes at any time

▶ draw shapes and lines in different colours, and use different colours and patterns for filling different parts of the drawing.

A selection of popular drawing packages, some of which have been used to produce artwork in this book.

You choose the tools and colours by pointing the cursor at icons (an **icon** is a little symbol or patch of colour) positioned around the edges of the screen. You can also choose some tools from menus which appear when you point at their names.

A picture produced by a drawing package is not stored in the same way as one produced by a painting package. Most drawing packages treat each shape you draw as a separate **object** and store its particular characteristics separately. You can alter the size of these objects easily and move them around on the screen.

The picture in Figure 5.2 has been drawn using some of the ready-made shapes available in a drawing package and some freehand drawing. You can make a drawing like this using a pointing device such as a **mouse**. It takes practice to be able to use a mouse quickly and accurately but you can remove any mistakes using the eraser tool. Once you have finished your drawing you can save it on disk so that you can use it again later. You can also print it out on a suitable printer. If you print a colour picture on a printer which can only produce black and white images, the picture will come out with a different pattern for each colour in the drawing. If you use a colour printer you should get a fairly good colour match between the picture on the screen and the printed picture (they probably won't look exactly the same because the colours are produced in different ways on the screen and on the paper).

Figure 5.2 *This drawing was produced by combining the ready-made shapes available in a drawing package with freehand lines.*

MAKING A DRAWING

When you make a drawing on your computer, you will probably want to use a mixture of ready-made shapes and freehand drawing.

Copying objects
If you want to repeat a shape in the drawing, you only need to draw it once – then you can make extra copies of it using your package's copy or **duplicate** facility (most drawing packages have this). You can then move the copies wherever you want them on the screen.

Changing the size of objects
Your drawing package will almost certainly let you change the size of the objects in your drawing. If your package lets you do this you might find it easiest to draw the shapes quite big and then shrink them to the size you want them to be. Most packages have a magnify or zoom facility to allow you to draw fine details accurately.

Overlapping objects
Getting different parts of your drawing to overlap properly requires some thought and planning. If the package is fairly simple you might have to build up your drawing starting from the background and adding the objects towards the front of the picture.

Correcting mistakes
Whatever you are drawing, you are bound to make some mistakes! You can usually remove the last mistake you've made using the

Figure 5.3 A more complicated drawing prepared using the copy and graded filling features available in a drawing package to give a three-dimensional effect.

'undo' command, provided you do this straight away but if you've drawn something else since you made the mistake, 'undo' probably won't work. You can use the 'erase' tool to rub out the part that's wrong, but this will leave a hole in the background and you'll have to redraw that part. The most sensible way to get round this problem is to save your work frequently. If you do this, and you make a big mistake, you can always go back to the last correct drawing you saved on the disk, which means you won't have to redraw the whole picture.

Layers

More advanced drawing packages allow you to work on different **layers** in a picture. You can draw each layer separately then put them together to produce the final drawing. In packages like this the various parts of the drawing are objects.

Grouping objects

In the drawing of the caterpillar and toadstools (Figure 5.2), each segment of the caterpillar body, the stalks and knobs of its feelers, each eye and its mouth are all separate objects. These objects were put into a single **group** once the caterpillar had been assembled. Grouping allows the whole caterpillar to be moved around and resized as if it was one object.

When we drew Figure 5.2, we kept the completed caterpillar in the front layer of the picture. The two toadstools were drawn freehand, the objects that made them up were grouped and then placed in the back layer of the picture so the caterpillar could be positioned in front of one of them.

We have used some of the features just described to draw the bunch of grapes in Figure 5.3. We drew one grape and one leaf then made more of them using copy, and arranged them so they overlapped. Some of the leaves had to be rotated first, then dragged into place using the mouse. We altered some of the colours to make the front leaves look paler than the back ones. Colouring a shape is called filling it. We also **graded** the fills to help the grapes look rounder. This works because each fill starts from a small pale area and becomes darker towards the edges of the shape.

Questions

What is a 'graphic'?
Write down the name of a drawing and painting package that you use in school.

Make a list of the ready-made shapes that are available in your package.

Make a list of the other tools and facilities which are available with this package.

Questions cont'd

Use newspapers and magazines to cut out and collect different examples of company logos. For each logo try to answer the following questions.

Are colours used? If so, how many are used?
Does it contain a picture or just text?
Is there a connection between the logo and what the company does?
Is it a simple or a complicated design?
Is it a design which will be easily recognised?
Do you think it's a successful logo?
What are the features which make a successful logo design?

Use a drawing and painting package, plus what you have found out about successful logos, to design a logo for your school.

Using computer aided design (CAD) packages

CAD packages are designed to make it easier to produce detailed plans and accurate technical drawings. Your package will probably have the following features:

▸ sets of ready-made symbols for standard types of drawings – such as electrical circuits

▸ standard ready-made shapes as tools for you to use

▸ it will allow you to use different types of line for drawing

▸ it can automatically round the corners of shapes

▸ it will let you fill shapes with ready-made shading patterns or patterns you have designed yourself.

A CAD package can also be used to carry out calculations. It can calculate the actual length of lines from a scale, and work out the actual areas of shapes which have been drawn to scale. The drawing in Figure 5.4 was produced using a CAD package.

CAD packages are designed for detailed work and it is important that the screen **resolution** of your computer system is good enough to show this detail. Resolution is the number of separate points, across and down, which can be displayed. Output to the printer or plotter is also detailed and very accurate and some printers can't achieve this degree of accuracy. You should check what your printer or plotter can do before starting on a detailed drawing.

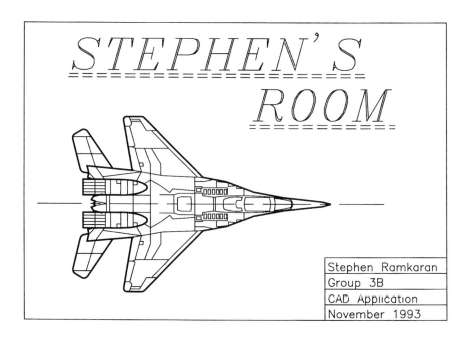

Figure 5.4   The sort of graphic you can draw using a CAD package.

What do the initials CAD stand for?

What type of drawings are best carried out using a CAD package?

What are the features of a CAD package which make it suitable for these types of drawings?

Choosing the right package

When you are doing graphics work it is important that you select a suitable package for the task you have to carry out.

▸ If you want colour, shading and lots of fills then choose an art or painting or drawing package.

▸ If you want detailed and accurate line drawings then choose a CAD package.

Summary

● Graphics packages are designed to be used for drawing. They are not usually very good at handling lots of text.

● Graphics packages have ready-made shapes (called tools) which you can use to help make the drawing you need.

● Freehand drawing with a mouse is not easy! Save your work regularly so if you do make a mistake you can go back to the last correct version.

- In a drawing package, once you have drawn an object you can make extra copies of it and rotate them or move them around on the screen. This can make it a lot easier to produce a detailed drawing.

- CAD packages are intended for producing plans and technical drawings. Using a CAD package you can produce very accurate and detailed drawings.

- A CAD package provides tools and features not found in ordinary graphics packages.

- CAD packages can be used to calculate lengths and areas. They can also measure angles.

- To get the best out of a CAD package takes time and requires a high resolution screen and printer.

SKILLS

When you have completed the work in this chapter you should be able to:

- Choose the appropriate type of graphics package for a particular task.

- Produce pictures using each type of package.

- Save your pictures and reload them for further work.

- Use the tools in your package to make drawing tasks as easy as possible.

- Using your drawing package, or your CAD package, make sensible use of layers and grouping of objects to build up drawings.

CHAPTER

Communicating Information –
Desktop publishing

■ *What can DTP do?*

Using desktop publishing (DTP) software you can design page layouts and combine text and graphics in almost any way you choose. You can also very easily rearrange parts of a page to try out different ideas. Some packages work only in black and white but some allow you to use colour. Your DTP package will provide at least these features:

▶ a good range of fonts in a variety of sizes

▶ basic text entry and editing facilities

▶ some drawing facilities

▶ it will allow you to import text from a variety of word processing programs

▶ you should also be able to import files produced by various painting and drawing packages or files created by scanning images using a **scanner** like the one in the photograph

A scanner for scanning images onto a computer screen.

you will probably find that the package also has a collection of pictures in various sizes ready for you to use. These pictures are called **clip-art** and can be put onto your page wherever you want them. You can see some examples of clip-art in Figure 6.1.

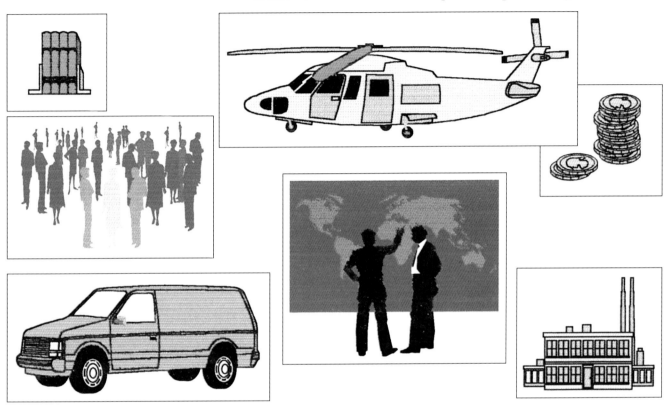

Figure 6.1 *Some examples of clip-art.*

What does 'importing' mean when we are talking about DTP packages?

What is a font? Find out the names of some different fonts and note the ones that the DTP package in your school has.

Getting started

Before you set up your page you will need to do some design work. You will need to make the following decisions:

▶ What information do you want to get across? (Is it a story, a set of instructions, a news article?)

▶ Who do you expect to read the finished page? (Friends or strangers? Experts or beginners? Children or adults?)

▶ Where and how will the page be read? (In class with a teacher? On a bus journey to work? At home in leisure time?)

All of these will influence the way you design your page. You will find it helps to make a few notes about these things early on so that later you can check that the pages you produce do what you set out to achieve.

Planning the page

STEP 1: DECIDING ON THE BASIC PLAN

You will need to make some decisions about how the page is going to be laid out. Figure 6.2 shows some possible layouts you could use.

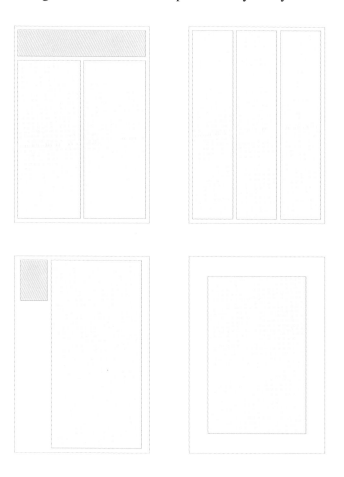

Figure 6.2 *Examples of layouts possible in portrait orientation.*

If you are producing a newsletter then you will probably choose a layout with several columns, partly because this layout is traditional for newsletters, but mainly because narrow columns are easy to skim through to find topics of interest. You must be realistic and remember that people will probably not read everything in your newsletter.

If you are presenting advertising material it must make a quick impact. A poster or leaflet must put its message across at the first glance if it is going to be successful. You will need to use large fonts and illustrations on a poster, so a column layout wouldn't work very well. Remember, people will probably not spend long reading what you produce. Keep it fairly simple and short.

The next figure shows some examples of advertising material. Some of them are very effective but others are not so good. Try to work out the good and bad features of each of them.

Figure 6.3 Good (and not so good) examples of advertising material.

Sometimes we need to make a quick impact at first sight, but also need to provide quite a lot of detailed information – for example, in a publicity leaflet for a theme park. In addition to this, the number of pages we can use might be limited because of the cost. A great deal can be achieved using just one sheet of paper. If we turn the page sideways (this is called **landscape** orientation – this page is printed in **portrait** orientation) then divide it into columns, we can produce a page which folds into three sections. The column that forms the 'front cover' of this leaflet can be used to make immediate impact and the inside columns and back cover can contain more detailed information. You can see how this works in Figure 6.4.

Side 1

Side 2

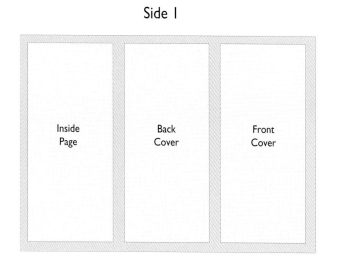
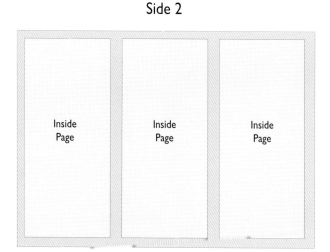

Figure 6.4 *The way columns are laid out to produce a folded leaflet.*

If you use this kind of layout for a leaflet then you will need to be very careful in deciding what information to put in each column to make the best impression, but the result can be worth the extra effort. You can fold paper in other ways as well – some are shown in Figure 6.5. Use some sheets of paper to try to work out other ways of folding it.

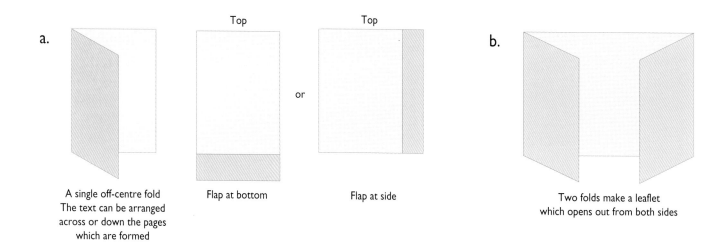

Figure 6.5 *Ways of folding one sheet of paper.*

If your finished publication is going to be several pages long then it's a good idea to try, as far you can, to keep the same style of layout all the way through, otherwise the overall effect can be very confusing and off-putting. If you do need to change the style of layout, keep the changes to a minimum.

STEP 2: ADDING TEXT AND GRAPHICS

Once you have completed your basic plan, it is time to work out where the text and illustrations will go and what information each item will communicate. Remember, the **white space** (empty space with nothing printed on it) of a page is just as important as the written material and pictures in creating impact. You don't have to fill every bit of the page – leave gaps between blocks of text and around pictures so that they will show up better.

Before you start to set up the page on the computer you should draw some plans to show what it will look like. Start with small plans (like those in Figure 6.6) and draw in the areas you intend to fill with text and pictures. You don't need to write in the words, just use shading or lines. If you intend to use colour in the final product then put this on your plan so you can see the impact. Try several ideas then produce a full-size plan (you can see one in Figure 6.7) and look at it to evaluate the effect of the layout itself, without any information in it.

HEADER	
PICTURE	SUB-HEADER
	PARAGRAPH
SUB-HEADER	SUB-HEADER
PARAGRAPH	PICTURE
SUB-HEADER	
PARAGRAPH	
SUB-HEADER	PARAGRAPH
PARAGRAPH	

HEADER	
PICTURE	PICTURE
	SUB-HEADER
SUB-HEADER	PARAGRAPH
PARAGRAPH	
SUB-HEADER	PARAGRAPH
PARAGRAPH	
PARAGRAPH	SUB-HEADER
	PARAGRAPH

HEADER	PICTURE
PARAGRAPH	
	SUB-HEADER
SUB-HEADER	PARAGRAPH
PARAGRAPH	PICTURE
SUB-HEADER	SUB-HEADER
PARAGRAPH	PARAGRAPH

Figure 6.6 *Possible designs for page layouts.*

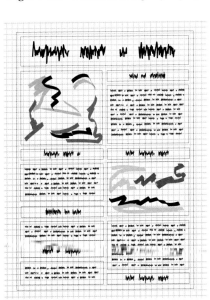

Figure 6.7 *The rough design for the newsletter.*

In the design sheet in Figure 6.7, black lines have been used to indicate text, and shading to indicate pictures. Large fonts are shown by thick black blocks. Don't be tempted to write in the words – at this stage you need to look at the layout on its own.

STEP 3: PREPARING THE TEXT

There are two approaches to the task of preparing the text. Whichever method you use, when you prepare your text, keep your readers in mind. Think about the words you are using and the message they are putting across. Don't pad things out just to fill up space.

Importing text from a word processor

You can use a suitable word processing package to type in and edit the text, save the text on disk, and then import it into the page in your DTP package. This is usually the easiest option if there is a lot of text because editing is usually much easier in the word processing package than in the DTP software.

If you use a word processor, try to avoid using anything that is not straightforward text. Don't alter the margins or use special fonts or styles. Use left justification so that the spaces between the words will all be the same size. You can adjust these things later in the DTP package – if you do them in the word processor then you might have problems importing the file into the DTP package.

At this stage you must check that you have saved the text file in a way that is acceptable to the DTP package you are using. Different packages save text in different ways, called **file formats**. You will need to find out what file formats the DTP package accepts and which ones your word processor can produce when you save work on disk. The three letters after the full stop in the file name may need to match. If you save your text file in a format the DTP package can't use then it will either not import it at all, or it will be imported but won't make sense. Choose a format that both packages can use and always save your text files in this format.

You will find it easiest to work with your text if you separate it into sensible sections – if your finished page is going to have two completely separate blocks of text then save each block of text in a separate file. Use a sensible naming system for your files as you can end up using several files and you might not always remember what is in them!

Working directly in the DTP package

The second approach to preparing text for DTP is to type it directly onto the page using the DTP software. This works well for headings and short sections of text but most DTP packages are not designed for editing lots of text and it can be a problem. If you intend to use this method then you should work out what the text will be and where it is to go before you start to type so you don't have to change or edit it very much.

Look at a typical page from your favourite magazine. Describe the layout of this page – the size and number of the columns, the size of the text. Draw a diagram (similar to the style of Figure 6.6) to show this layout.

What proportion of the page is taken up by:

small text (body text)?
graphics?
headings?
white space?

How does the page design draw the reader's attention to various items?

Repeat the exercise using a magazine aimed at a different market.

Compare the two layouts you have looked at. How is each layout appropriate for the readers that magazine is aimed at?

The company logo of Hodder Headline plc.

PREPARING GRAPHICS

We use graphics on a page for several reasons – but remember, don't use graphics just to fill leftover space!

▶ Graphics – graphs, maps and diagrams – can often give information much more clearly than a description in words.

▶ Describing something realistically is sometimes hard to do in words – photographs do this very well.

▶ You can often appeal to people's feelings more effectively using a careful selection of graphics than by using words – again, photographs usually work best.

▶ Including graphics can break up your page and make the whole document much more interesting to the reader.

▶ A graphic can become associated with a particular company. The company can then use it to promote their image and their products. This kind of graphic is often called a logo.

Preparing your graphic

Once you have decided why you want to include a graphic, you need to prepare it. If it is a line drawing you could draw it using a suitable graphics package, as we saw in Chapter 5, and produce a file ready for importing into the DTP package. As with text, you need to be careful to save your graphic in a file format that your DTP package can use. If you find it hard to produce a reasonable drawing like this you could use clip-art.

Pictures can be converted to images on a computer screen.

You can also **scan** a picture and produce a file ready to import onto the page that way. A scanner measures the light reflected from a picture working from one edge to the other. The scanner software uses these measurements to produce an image on the screen and you can save this in a file on disk. If you choose to scan a drawing you will almost certainly need to tidy up the scanned image before you can use it. The scanner software will let you do this but it can take a very long time.

If you want to include photographs you will have to use a scanner to produce the necessary files. Photographs can be difficult to scan successfully. You might need to try a few times, varying the scanner settings, before you are satisfied with the result. Occasionally you get a better result if you photocopy the original photograph and then scan the copy.

STEP 4: PUTTING THE PAGE TOGETHER

You then use your DTP package to put all the elements together. A DTP package can be either page-based or document-based.

A **document-based package** is good for working on several pages, all with the same basic layout. You can set up the layout as a master page then add extra pages, with the same basic layout, as you need them. This type of package lets imported text which won't all fit on one page flow onto the next page, so you don't have to worry about the length of text files.

A **page-based package** is more flexible if you need to change the layout from one page to the next, but if the text is too long for the space available it won't automatically be continued on the next page.

Preparing a page template

Most DTP packages need you to set up columns and boxes (called **frames**) for the text and graphics to go into before you can put anything else on the page. It is very easy to move the frames and their contents around on the page or to change their size to make everything fit properly. Find out about the package you will be using and try setting up your own page plan – the **page template**.

When you have set up all the boxes your page template will probably look something like the one in Figure 6.8. You are now ready to put your text and graphics into the page.

Putting in the text

To add text from a text file select the first frame to be filled and choose the font you want to use if necessary. Give the command to import a text file (this is sometimes called a **story**). Enter the name of the text file you want to use – and if everything goes right the text will be loaded. It might appear straight away in the selected box or you may need to use another command to insert the text on the page, depending on the package you're using. You can now alter the font and size of the text as you want.

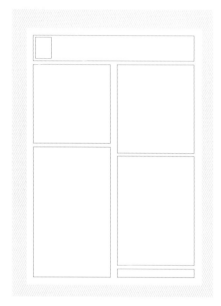

Figure 6.8 *The page template used for the newsletter showing frames. These will be the same in every issue.*

You will probably want to type some of the text straight onto the page. In most packages, to do this you select the box, position, and the font you want and start typing. Some packages use a separate **text editor** (like a simple word processor) and then you must give an 'edit text' command before you can do anything to your text. In this sort of package you will put the text onto the page using another command. In Figure 6.9 some text has been put into the basic page template we saw in Figure 6.8.

Figure 6.9 Some of the text has been inserted into one frame of the template.

Putting in graphics

Putting your graphics on the page is very like putting in text. Select the box, give the 'load picture' command, enter the file name of your graphic and your picture should load straight into the page. Be patient – this could take some time if the picture is large. You may need to adjust the size of the frame if it's not the same shape as the picture. If you find the picture is long and thin, shorten or widen the frame until it looks right, if it's short and fat, lengthen the frame or make it narrower. You can stretch pictures deliberately to create a special effect. Figure 6.10 shows the page we saw earlier with a graphic in place. The final page, with all the text and graphics in place is shown in Figure 6.11.

Figure 6.10 The newsletter first page, with a graphic imported into one of the frames as well as some text.

Figure 6.11 The final page, with all the text and graphics in place.

A. Text aligned to picture
B. Text rotated vertically
C. Image imported and scaled

Figure 6.12 You can produce special effects using DTP packages – here are a few.

Special effects

If you want text to flow around a graphic then you must make sure that you put the graphic on the page before the text. To find out how to do this and how to produce other special effects, you will need to read the instructions supplied with your DTP package. You should be able to add borders with shadows to frames and also overlap frames if you want. The page in Figure 6.12 shows some of the special effects you can get using DTP.

Write down the stages you go through as you create a document in DTP.

For the DTP package which you use in school, write down the commands you need or the method you use to:

> create a frame
> resize a frame
> move a frame
> delete a frame
> enter text straight into a frame
> import text
> import a graphic
> alter the font style of a section of text
> alter the font size of a section of text
> resize a graphic
> save a document
> print a document.

STEP 5: PRINTING THE PAGE

When you have completed your page *and you have saved it on disk*, you are ready to print it out. You must *always* **save** your work before trying to **print** it – if anything is going to go wrong, printing is the stage when it is most likely to happen and if you haven't saved your page you could lose all your hard work!

The quality of the output you get will depend on the type of printer you are using. Laser and inkjet printers will produce very good output. Your package will probably be able to send output to several different types of printer. You might need to select the right kind before giving the print command. The way you do this will depend on the package you are using so you will have to find out.

The finished product. All of these leaflets were produced using DTP packages.

Summary

- A DTP package lets you lay out pages in any way you want.

- It provides a range of fonts in a variety of sizes.

- Graphics can be put anywhere on the page.

- You should design the page before putting it together.

- The text and graphics can be prepared using other packages then imported into the page.

- Clip-art is available with many DTP packages and can be used as ready-made illustrations.

- Various special effects can be produced.

■ *Suggestions for DTP work*

- Produce an advertisement for a school play, concert or sporting event.
- Produce a class newspaper.
- Produce a leaflet giving information about one of your hobbies to encourage others to try it.
- Produce a sheet to tell strangers how to get to your school from outside your town.
- Produce fact sheets about how to stay healthy. You could concentrate on healthy eating, exercise or the dangers of smoking.

SKILLS

When you have completed the work in this chapter you should be able to:

- Design layouts for pages for particular purposes.
- Select suitable graphics for the page.
- Set up the page template using the DTP software.
- Import text and graphics and arrange them on the page.
- Save, retrieve and print pages.

Questions

1 Here is the menu for a wedding breakfast.

> Menu
>
> Cream of mushroom soup
>
> Roast sirloin of beef
>
> Sauté potatoes
>
> A selection of seasonal vegetables or salad
>
> (for vegetarians - Casserole of three beans with mixed vegetables)
>
> Lemon syllabub and ratafia biscuits
>
> Cheese board
>
> Coffee

MEG sample material

You have been asked to use the features of a word processor or DTP package to improve the appearance of this menu card. Suggest at least five improvements you would make.

CHAPTER

7 Communicating Information – Sound

C omputers can be made to generate and recognise different sounds, using **peripheral devices** such as loudspeakers and microphones connected to the computer and controlled by the computer's software (as shown in the photograph).

Sound can be produced from a computer using loudspeakers and controlled on screen.

■ *Storing sounds*

T he loudness of sounds varies on a smooth, continuous scale, between very quiet and very loud. In the same way, the **pitch** of sounds varies continuously between very low and very high. This kind of continuous variation is called **analogue** variation. When values change in distinct steps rather than on a smooth scale we say that the values are **digital**. Computers can only work with digital values, so to handle sound using a computer we must change the pattern of the sound from analogue to digital values when the sound is input and its pattern is stored. The stored digital values can be used to generate sound from the computer, through the loudspeakers. Figure 7.1 shows the analogue pattern of loudness of a sound over a fraction of a second, and Figure 7.2 shows the digital pattern of the same sound. You can see the continuous lines in the first pattern and the separate steps in the second pattern.

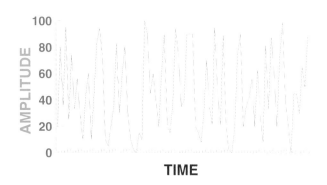

Figure 7.1 *A sound signal with continuously varying amplitude (loudness). This is an analogue signal.*

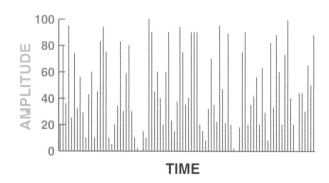

Figure 7.2 *The same sound signal as in the last figure, shown as a digital sound.*

Many modern computers have a speaker built in to the system. Sound can be generated through this speaker, but the quality of the sound often leaves a lot to be desired. Better quality sounds can be produced by **sampling** the sound, storing the samples on disk and then playing them back – but standard computers don't usually have the parts to do this. Even a short sound sequence needs a lot of stored data. Storing very large samples can take up a vast amount of memory and disk space. Playing back these samples needs extra **chips** and circuits inside the computer and better speakers than are usually built into a standard computer system.

Computers that have special sound hardware can store sounds inputted through a microphone and can play them back. Software can be used to combine and distort these samples in lots of ways to make new sounds which can be played back through high-quality speakers. Sampled sounds are often used in computer games, but you only hear them properly if you play the game on a computer with the extra hardware and speakers.

Sampling sound

Y ou can sample sound by connecting a microphone to the computer system and creating the sounds you want. This has some limitations, because any stray sound in the room – like a chair being moved, someone coughing, or even breathing noises – will also be picked up and stored by the computer.

If a computer has the right kind of connection (a **MIDI interface**) then, with the right software, sound produced on an electronic keyboard can be sampled directly, cutting out the problem of stray noise. When you sample a sound the analogue values of the sound are converted into digital values for the computer to store. This has to be done many thousands of times a second to make sure that the quality of the sound is as much like the original as possible – this is why sampling needs so much memory in the computer and storage space on disk.

Any kind of sound can be sampled using a microphone – not just speech and music. Once a sound has been sampled and its pattern stored, it can be replayed by converting the digital pattern stored on disk back into sound played through a speaker system.

Mixing and distortion

Sounds that have been sampled can be altered in various ways by using special computer software. It is possible to **mix** several different samples. For example, if you need a farmyard sound you could sample pig, sheep and cow sounds separately then combine them to make a background noise of animals. You could combine this mix with other sounds (such as tractor noises or speech) to produce the final effect of a busy farmyard.

One obvious use of sound mixing is in producing sound tracks for films. Special effects, such as noises for aliens and dinosaurs, have been produced for many films by mixing and **distorting** sampled sounds. Mixing and some distortion is used in recording music as well, producing effects that can't be produced on any musical instrument.

Music recording studio using sampling.

Sequencing

Sequencing sounds is deciding the order in which to play sound samples. In the example of the farm we used earlier, you might not want all the sounds at the same time – you might want the animal noises first, then the tractor and the farmer. You can set up this sequence by setting the order in which the samples are to be used. You can repeat very short sequences to produce special effects as well – for example, repeating the middle section of a short squeal several times will turn it into a long howl.

Working with sound

If you want to work with sound, you should check what the computer systems available to you can do. If the hardware can do what you want (and if the special software packages are available) you will be able to sample and store sounds and to combine and distort them. The sounds can then be played back as required. Multimedia software will let you attach particular stored sounds to pictures or actions.

Summary

- Sounds can be sampled and stored using a computer system.
- Stored sounds can be replayed unchanged.
- Sound samples can be combined and altered to produce new sounds.
- Storage of sound data can take quite a lot of disk space because to get good quality the sound characteristics must be captured thousands of times a second.
- Getting good-quality sound out of a computer system requires extra hardware (such as speakers) and extra chips and circuits in the computer.

SKILLS

When you have completed the work in this chapter, providing you have the right hardware and software, you should be able to:

- Sample sounds.
- Play back sampled sounds.
- Mix different sounds.
- Organise sequences of sounds.

Questions

1 What is meant by:

  a sampling
  b distorting
  c mixing of sound?

2 How could sound be used effectively in each of the following situations?

  a In presenting information on screen about events at a school open day.
  b As part of a word-processing package.
  c As part of a multimedia presentation about zoo animals.

In each case explain what kind of sound you would want to use and how this sound would be produced.

Spreadsheets

You can use a **spreadsheet** to carry out calculations. A spreadsheet is useful because you can do lots of calculations and use the answers you get to work out other things in the same spreadsheet. Once you have set up your spreadsheet you can change some of the numbers and it will work out the new answers for you. When you have all your answers on the screen you can print out your work, with all the headings and explanations you have included. You can save your work on disk so you can finish it later or in case you want to use the same spreadsheet for new sets of data.

■ *Spreadsheet basics*

A spreadsheet is a grid, which looks like a table, divided into columns and rows. Each **cell** in the grid can be identified by the column it is in and the row it is in – this is called the **cell address** (you can see this in Figure 8.1). For example, the address B3 means the cell is in column B and in the third row.

	A	B	C	D	E	F	G	H
1								
2								
3								
4								
5								

Figure 8.1   An empty spreadsheet, showing columns, rows and cells.

Cells can contain text, numbers or **formulae**. You use text for headings and labels to make things clearer. The numbers you put into the spreadsheet are used to carry out calculations. You use formulae to tell the computer how to calculate the answers you want. The formula contains the address of each cell used in the calculation and any fixed numbers you need – you can see an example of a formula in Figure 8.2.

Figure 8.2   An example of a spreadsheet formula.

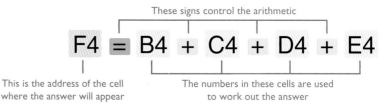

What three items can a cell in a spreadsheet contain? Give an explanation and an example of each of these items.

What do we mean by a cell address? Give an example of a cell address from the spreadsheet package you use at school.

The formula in Figure 8.2 adds together the contents of cells B4, C4, D4 and E4 and puts the answer in cell F4. Arithmetic in spreadsheets uses these signs:

- $+$ for addition
- $-$ for subtraction
- $*$ for multiplication
- $/$ for division
- $\wedge$ for raising to a power (exponentiation) – for example, 2^3 means 2^3

If you put part of the formula in brackets, that part will be worked out before any other parts.

Figure 8.3 is a spreadsheet that has been used to work out how much television time was used for different types of programme in one week. The printout shows the formulae instead of the answers.

	A	B	C	D	E	F	G	H
1	DAY	CHANNEL	SPORT	FILM	SOAPS	CHILDRENS	NEWS	HRS TRANSMITTED
2								
3	Monday	BBC1						=SUM(C3..G3)
4		BBC2						=SUM(C4..G4)
5		ITV						=SUM(C5..G5)
6		CH4						=SUM(C6..G6)
7								
8	Tuesday	BBC1						=SUM(C8..G8)
9		BBC2						=SUM(C9..G9)
10		ITV						=SUM(C10..G10)
11		CH4						=SUM(C11..G11)
12								
13	Wednesday	BBC1						=SUM(C13..G13)
14		BBC2						=SUM(C14..G14)
15		ITV						=SUM(C15..G15)
16		CH4						=SUM(C16..G16)
17								
18	Thursday	BBC1						=SUM(C18..G18)
19		BBC2						=SUM(C19..G19)
20		ITV						=SUM(C20..G20)
21		CH4						=SUM(C21..G21)
22								
23	Friday	BBC1						=SUM(C23..G23)
24		BBC2						=SUM(C24..G24)
25		ITV						=SUM(C25..G25)
26		CH4						=SUM(C26..G26)
27								
28	Saturday	BBC1						=SUM(C28..G28)
29		BBC2						=SUM(C29..G29)
30		ITV						=SUM(C30..G30)
31		CH4						=SUM(C31..G31)
32								
33	Sunday	BBC1						=SUM(C33..G33)
34		BBC2						=SUM(C34..G34)
35		ITV						=SUM(C35..G35)
36		CH4						=SUM(C36..G36)
37								
38								
39								
40	Total		=SUM(C3..C36)	=SUM(D3..D36)	=SUM(E3..E36)	=SUM(F3..F36)	=SUM(G3..G36)	=SUM(H3..H36)
41								
42	% OF TOTAL TRANSMISSION		=SUM(C40/$H40)*100	=SUM(D40/$H40)*100	=SUM(E40/$H40)*100	=SUM(F40/$H40)*100	=SUM(G40/$H40)*100	=SUM(H40/$H40)*100

Figure 8.3 *Spreadsheet of television programmes, showing the formulae.*

Figure 8.4 is the same spreadsheet, printed out to show the answers.

	A	B	C	D	E	F	G	H
1	DAY	CHANNEL	SPORT	FILM	SOAPS	CHILDRENS	NEWS	HRS TRANSMITTED
2								
3	Monday	BBC1	2.0	1.5	3.0	2.0	2.0	10.5
4		BBC2	2.0	1.0	3.0	0.0	2.0	8.0
5		ITV	2.0	1.0	3.0	0.0	2.0	8.0
6		CH4	2.0	1.0	3.0	0.0	2.0	8.0
7								
8	Tuesday	BBC1	2.0	1.5	3.0	2.0	3.0	11.5
9		BBC2	1.0	1.5	0.0	1.5	1.0	5.0
10		ITV	1.0	1.5	0.0	1.5	1.0	5.0
11		CH4	1.0	1.5	0.0	1.5	1.0	5.0
12								
13	Wednesday	BBC1	2.0	1.5	3.0	3.0	3.0	12.5
14		BBC2	3.0	2.0	2.0	2.0	2.0	11.0
15		ITV	3.0	2.0	2.0	2.0	2.0	11.0
16		CH4	3.0	2.0	2.0	2.0	2.0	11.0
17								
18	Thursday	BBC1	2.0	1.0	3.0	0.0	2.0	8.0
19		BBC2	1.0	0.0	3.0	3.0	0.0	7.0
20		ITV	1.0	0.0	3.0	3.0	0.0	7.0
21		CH4	1.0	0.0	3.0	3.0	0.0	7.0
22								
23	Friday	BBC1	2.0	1.5	3.0	0.0	2.0	8.5
24		BBC2	2.0	1.5	3.0	2.0	3.0	11.5
25		ITV	2.0	1.5	3.0	2.0	3.0	11.5
26		CH4	2.0	1.5	3.0	2.0	3.0	11.5
27								
28	Saturday	BBC1	2.0	1.0	2.0	2.0	1.5	8.5
29		BBC2	3.0	1.0	3.0	2.0	1.5	10.5
30		ITV	3.0	1.0	3.0	2.0	1.5	10.5
31		CH4	2.0	1.0	3.0	0.0	2.0	8.0
32								
33	Sunday	BBC1	4.0	0.0	2.0	1.0	3.0	10.0
34		BBC2	4.0	0.0	2.0	1.0	3.0	10.0
35		ITV	2.0	1.5	3.0	2.0	3.0	11.5
36		CH4	2.0	1.0	3.0	0.0	2.0	8.0
37								
38								
39								
40	Total		40.0	31.0	70.0	41.5	54.5	257.0
41								
42	% OF TOTAL TRANSMISSION		23.3	12.1	27.2	16.1	21.2	100.0

Figure 8.4 *The same spreadsheet as in Figure 8.3, with the answers included in the printout.*

What your spreadsheet package can do

Different spreadsheet packages have different ways of showing what you want to put in a cell. For the spreadsheet package you are using, find out how to:

▶ put text into cells

▶ put numbers in a cell

▶ put a formula in a cell

▶ change the width of a column

▶ duplicate a formula

▶ print your spreadsheet.

You will probably find it useful to know how to duplicate a formula down a column or across a row. In our television programmes spreadsheet (Figure 8.3) the formula was put in cell F4. In the other rows we also needed to add up cells in the same columns as for F4 so we copied the formula down the column in a way that made the package change the row number for each row down the spreadsheet. So, in row 5 the formula became:

$$F5 = B5 + C5 + D5 + E5.$$

We can also copy cell addresses as they are.

Learning how to copy will save you lots of typing and, if you have complicated formulae, will help you to avoid mistakes.

You will need to know how to print your spreadsheet to show both data and formulae, so that people can see how you worked out your answers.

As you work with your spreadsheet package you will discover more about what it can do. You will be able to:

▶ change the cell format so that the contents are centred or on the left or the right

▶ make answers appear with a fixed number of decimal places

▶ you may be able to select data to produce graphs and charts that can be printed out.

Q

Write down the name of the spreadsheet package you use in school. Investigate and write down the commands you give or methods you use to:

    enter text into a cell
    enter a number into a cell
    enter a formula into a cell
    change the width of a column
    edit the contents of a cell
    change the cell format
save your spreadsheet
print out the spreadsheet showing contents
print out the spreadsheet showing the formulae used.

■ *Designing and setting up your own spreadsheet*

Before you can set up your spreadsheet you will need to think about what answers you want it to produce.

STEP 1

Decide the questions that need to be answered and the calculations you will need to carry out to get these answers.

STEP 2

Work out what data you will need to calculate the answers to your questions and collect the data.

You will probably need to do some research to collect the information that you need in order to get this data. In our spreadsheet example, the details about programme length and type were collected from television magazines.

STEP 3

Design the layout of the spreadsheet – you will need to work out what headings are needed and how wide the columns will have to be (remember headings tend to need more room than numbers).

When you start to design the layout it is a good idea to plan it out on squared paper because lots of layouts are possible and you need to decide which one will work best. You don't need to put in all the data but you should show what goes where and how to **format** it. Formatting includes the position of what goes in the cell and the number of decimal places. Put formulae in where they are needed but, where you will duplicate the formula all the way down a column, don't bother to write the formula in every cell in that column.

In designing your spreadsheet think about whether the data is grouped so that it is clear and whether it's easy to see the answers.

If you plan to draw graphs or charts with some data, keep the data and headings in groups – you won't be able to use data for a graph if the data is scattered all over the spreadsheet.

The design for the television programme spreadsheet can be seen in Figure 8.5.

STEP 4

Set up the spreadsheet on the computer. The first thing to do is to adjust the **column widths** so that everything will fit in. When you've done this, put in the headings – these will help you get the data in the right places.

	A	B	C	D	E	F	G	H	
1	DAY	CHANNEL	SPORT	FILM	SOAPS	CHILDRENS	NEWS	HRS TRANSMITTED	
2									
3	Monday	BBC1							
4		BBC2							
5		ITV							
6		CH4							
7									
8	Tuesday	BBC1							
9		BBC2							
10		ITV							
11		CH4							
12									
13	Wednesday	BBC1							
14		BBC2							
15		ITV							
16		CH4							
17									
18	Thursday	BBC1							
19		BBC2							
20		ITV							
21		CH4							
22									
23	Friday	BBC1							
24		BBC2							
25		ITV							
26		CH4							
27									
28	Saturday	BBC1							
29		BBC2							
30		ITV							
31		CH4							
32									
33	Sunday	BBC1							
34		BBC2							
35		ITV							
36		CH4							
37									
38									
39									
40	Total		=SUM(C3:C36)						
41									
42	% of total transmission		=(C40/$H40)*100						
43									
44									
45									

All data in these columns is numeric, uses 1 decimal place and is right justified

Duplicate formulae across (relative)

Duplicate this formula across as well – note that cell H40 is an ABSOLUTE cell address and won't be changed. Cell C40 will be changed as it is duplicated.

Figure 8.5 *The design for the television programme spreadsheet.*

Set up the formulae in the cells and save your spreadsheet on disk. Don't forget to give it a sensible name and make a note of the name you use.

Now put in the data. If your spreadsheet is set to automatically recalculate, so that it always works out answers straight away, the answers will appear in the cells with formulae in them. Once you have put in all the data, save your work again with a different name.

You can now use the spreadsheet to produce any graphs you need. The bar chart in Figure 8.6 was produced from our television programmes spreadsheet. It shows how the time used for each type of programme differs for different channels.

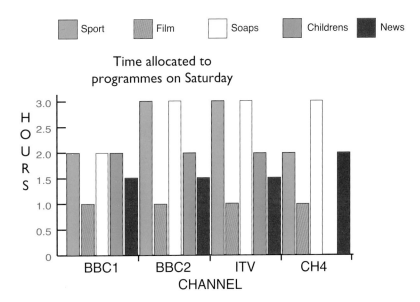

Figure 8.6 *A bar chart produced from the database, showing how the time for each type of programme differs.*

You will probably also need to print out the spreadsheet to show what you have found out.

Summary

- Spreadsheets can be used to carry out calculations.

- In a spreadsheet the **data** is entered by the user.

- A spreadsheet contains formulae – the rules for working out the answers from the data.

- Spreadsheets also contain text to put the data into context so that it becomes **information** for the user.

- In some packages, data from spreadsheets can be used to produce graphs and charts.

SKILLS

When you have completed the work in this chapter you should be able to:

- Design a simple spreadsheet.

- Use your spreadsheet package to set up a spreadsheet.

- Put data into your spreadsheet.

- Read the answers from your spreadsheet.

- Produce graphs and charts from spreadsheet data.

Questions

1 How is a single location in a spreadsheet identified?

2 The spreadsheet below is used to store details of stock in a shop's stock control system:

	A	B	C	D	E	F	G	H
1	STOCK	NAME	SIZE	STOCK	SELLING	VALUE	MINIMUM	NO. ABOVE
2	NO.			LEVEL	PRICE		STOCK	MINIMUM
3							LEVEL	
4								
5	0234	Baked beans	420 g	127	0.36	45.72	24	103
6	0245	Beefburgers	12 pack	36	1.98	71.20	12	24
7	0367	Lentils	500 g	45	0.45	20.25	12	33
8	0478	Long grain rice	1000 g	70	1.46	102.2	25	45
9	0579	Peaches	550 g	36	0.78	28.08	12	24

a Which locations would have to be changed if a new delivery of baked beans arrived?

b Name two locations containing numbers worked out using formulae.

c It would be useful if the spreadsheet showed the total value of the stock. How would you make it do this?

d Which location would you change if the price of rice went up by 5p? Which locations would change as a result of this?

3 A school runs several holiday trips each year and allows pupils to pay in money each week to meet the cost of the trip. Up to 40 pupils can go on each trip. Design a spreadsheet to hold pupil and payment information about one trip. Show clearly which locations contain headings, data and formulae and what formulae you would use.

4 You use a spreadsheet package to analyse the cost of a holiday in Australia.

a Write down one item of information which you want output.

b Write down two items of data you will enter on the spreadsheet.

c Give two items of data you should use to test if the results are reasonable.

5 Describe, using a diagram, how a model of a pupil's weekly finances could be constructed.

6 Fred has designed a spreadsheet to represent information about a number of personal stereo systems. Here is some test data for this spreadsheet:

MEG sample material

MEG sample material

I	A REF	B MAKE	C MODEL	D WEIGHT	E LENGTH	F WIDTH	G HEIGHT	H PRICE
2				(g)	(cm)	(cm)	(cm)	(£)
3	100	AIWA	HS-J470	245	9	12	35	105
4	109	SONY	WMD6C	640	18	4	10	260
5	113	KENWOOD	CPS-550	194	10	7	2	150
6	129	SANYO	ESP7	190	11	10	2	140
7	143	CROWN	WMT7R	250	11	7	2	30

ULEAC specimen material

Fred wants the average price of the stereo systems to appear in cell H8.

a What must Fred type into cell H8?

b The spreadsheet package that Fred uses can produce various charts and graphs. Fred wants to produce a bar chart of the weights of the personal stereos.
(i) Describe what Fred must do.
(ii) Name two other types of chart that the spreadsheet package might be able to produce.

c The size of each stereo is given as three dimensions (length, width, height). The volume of each stereo is found by calculating:

$$\text{length} \times \text{width} \times \text{height}$$

Show how Fred could extend the spreadsheet to display the volume of each stereo.

7 The spreadsheet below shows data on agriculture in the British Isles:

	A	B	C	D	E	
				%	%	%
I		COUNTRY	AGRICULTURE			
2		Name	Area	Grass	Arable	Fruit & Veg
3						
4		England				
5		Wales				
6		Scotland				
7		Ireland				
8						
9						

a Which cell would you use to put the total agricultural area?

b What formula would you put in that cell?

Questions cont'd

c The spreadsheet has the ability to produce the following types of graph:

Bar   Line   Pie   Scatter

Which one would be most suitable:
(i) For showing the proportions of grass, arable and fruit & veg for England?
(ii) To compare the agricultural areas for the four countries.
d If you want to add similar data for other countries, where could you find that data?

SEG specimen paper

CHAPTER 9

Using Spreadsheets for Modelling

■ *What is a computer model?*

A computer model contains data and rules. The rules control the way in which the model works. They are instructions for carrying out calculations, or conditions when particular calculations should be carried out. The model can be of a situation or a process. You can't use a spreadsheet to make a scale model of an object but you can use it to predict how that object will behave in certain situations. For example if you wanted to build a very strong container you could make a cardboard model to show its shape, but this model wouldn't be any use for predicting what would happen if the container fell off a lorry. A spreadsheet model of the container could contain data about the material the container is made from and rules (formulae) about how it would react to impact.

■ *Why use computer models?*

We use computer models to find out what will happen when we change a situation – without actually having to make these changes. For instance, we could investigate the effect of making the container walls different thicknesses without having to make lots of different containers and drop them off lorries.

This type of modelling has a number of advantages:

1   It's much cheaper to set up a computer model than to build a whole system for testing.
2   You can make changes quickly and easily in a computer model to find out what happens if the situation changes.

3 You can repeat your tests as often as you need to.

4 You can model dangerous situations safely (like testing car designs by 'crashing' them, without actually crashing a car).

5 If a test using a simulation or model goes badly wrong the consequences aren't disastrous – no-one gets hurt and it's not too expensive to try again.

But

You must remember that the computer model is not the real thing – a computer model can never *prove* that a system will work the same way in the real world. The answers or results that we get are only as reliable as the model we've created, and if we try to model very complex situations we can never take into account all the factors. This is especially true if humans are involved in the situation – for example a computer model of the operation of the Stock Market will probably be unreliable because the humans involved in share dealing often react in unpredictable ways.

Explain what we mean by a computer model.

Write down three different types of computer model. For each type give an example of a situation where it is used.

List four reasons why using computer models is better than using real systems to test different situations.

Types of computer model

Computer models include:

▶ *Mathematical models* using spreadsheet software – these are often used for modelling financial situations.

▶ *Simulation modelling* where the model (the simulator) is as close to the real thing as possible – like the flight simulators used in training pilots. (More about simulators in Chapter 10.)

Constructing a costing spreadsheet

In this section you are going to learn how to construct and use a simple spreadsheet model. We will take it step by step.

STEP 1: DESCRIBE THE SITUATION TO BE MODELLED

The example we will use here is a financial model which will let you find out the cost of making a single portion of cake.

Recipe Costing Sheet

	A	B	C	D	E	F	G
1							
2							
3	*Recipe for*	Fresh cream sponge cake					
4							
5	*Number of portions*			8			
6							
7	*Ingredient*	*Pack Size*		Cost of	Amount		Cost of this
8				Pack	Needed		amount
9							
10	margarine		500 g	0.58	100 g		=D10/B10*E10
11	sugar		1000 g	0.82	100 g		=D11/B11*E11
12	eggs		6 eggs	0.72	1 egg		=D12/B12*E12
13	S. R. flour		1500 g	0.56	125 g		=D13/B13*E13
14	milk		1000 ml	0.38	45 ml		=D14/B14*E14
15	cocoa		125 g	0.62	45 g		=D15/B15*E15
16	double cream		142 ml	0.39	142 ml		=D16/B16*E16
17							
18	Other Costs						
19							
20	Cooking Time		45.00 Mins				
21	Power Used	=1/60*B20	Units				
22	Cost per Unit		0.0812				
23	Cost of Baking	=B21*B22					
24							
25	Cost per Portion	=(SUM(G10..G16)+B23)/C5					

Figure 9.1 A financial model for making one slice of cake.

STEP 2: DECIDE WHAT QUESTIONS YOU WANT TO ANSWER

You want to find out:

▶ How cutting the cake into smaller or bigger pieces would affect the cost of a portion.

▶ How changing prices of ingredients affects the cost of a portion.

▶ How a change in energy costs affects the cost of a portion.

You could use the spreadsheet to answer other questions as well – can you think of more?

STEP 3: COLLECT THE INFORMATION YOU NEED TO GET THE DATA FOR THE SPREADSHEET

You need:

▶ A list of the ingredients in the cake.

▶ The amount of each ingredient you need.

▶ How much a pack of each ingredient costs.

▶ The size of each of the packs you would have to buy.

▶ The cost of a unit of electricity or gas.

▶ The number of portions of cake you expect to make.

You will find the ingredients list and quantities you need in a recipe book, the pack sizes and prices in your local supermarket and how much the electricity costs by looking at an electricity bill.

STEP 4: WORK OUT THE RULES FOR YOUR MODEL

You will use the rules that you work out to construct the formulae when you design the actual spreadsheet.

This model doesn't have too many rules.

Rule 1 The cost of ingredients in the cake is:

$$\frac{cost\ of\ the\ pack \times amount\ used}{amount\ in\ the\ pack}$$

Rule 2 The total cost of ingredients is the sum of the cost of each separate ingredient.

Rule 3 Power used is:

$$rating\ of\ oven\ in\ kW \times cooking\ time\ in\ hours$$

Rule 4 Cost of baking is:

$$power\ used \times cost\ of\ a\ unit\ of\ power$$

Rule 5 Cost of a portion is:

$$\frac{(total\ cost\ of\ ingredients + cost\ of\ baking)}{number\ of\ portions\ made}$$

STEP 5: DESIGN THE LAYOUT OF THE SPREADSHEET

It makes sense to plan out your spreadsheet on squared paper (just as you did when planning database reports in Chapter 3).

You must work out what headings you need so that your spreadsheet makes sense to anyone reading it. You should decide where all the data will go on the spreadsheet. As you decide what goes in each column, you will also have to think about how wide the columns should be (remember that headings usually need more space than numbers). Show where you will put the data but don't bother to write it all in on the plan.

You need to decide where in each cell you want your text and numbers to appear – you can justify it left or right or you can have the cell contents centred (look back at Chapter 4 for what these terms mean). You also need to decide on the number of decimal places you want displayed. If your quantities are in grams and millilitres then you can display these numbers as whole numbers, but the cells with costs in them will need to display two decimal places.

If you want to include units in your spreadsheet you will have to put them in separate columns next to the numbers. If you try to put them in with the numbers the package will treat the cell contents as text and won't work out the answers correctly. Once you have decided on the layout of your spreadsheet you can work out the formulae you need. You couldn't do this before because the formulae need cell addresses.

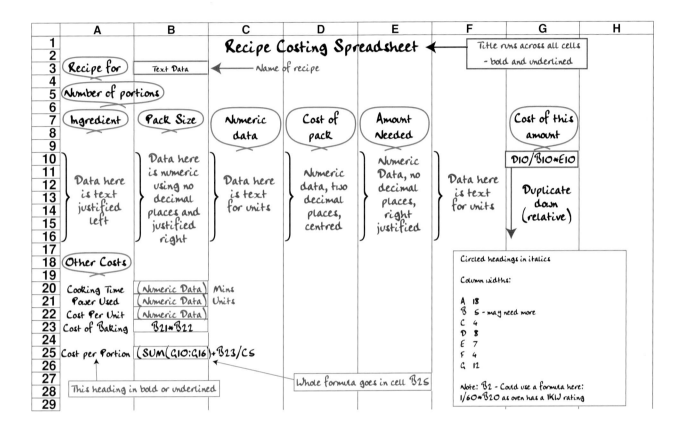

Figure 9.2 *The design for a spreadsheet to work out how much it would cost to produce a cake.*

You can see one way the recipe spreadsheet could be set up in Figure 9.2, but other layouts would work just as well. Notice that the formulae have already been put in to some of the cells. Cell G10 contains the formula:

$$=D10/B10*E10.$$

This is the formula for Rule 1 – the rule for working out how much the amount of a particular ingredient needed to make the cake costs. Cell D10 contains the cost of the packet of margarine. This is divided by the pack size, which is in B10, and is multiplied by the amount needed (which is in cell E10). In the design you only need to write this formula once because you'll be able to copy it into the other cells where it is needed by duplicating it down the column. The package will change the row numbers as it makes the extra copies.

The formula in cell B25 is different from the others. It uses a **function** to add up all the cells between G10 and G16. The function name is SUM. A function is a mathematical operation already set up

STEP 6: SET UP THE SPREADSHEET ON YOUR COMPUTER

Follow your design sheet carefully. You will need to alter column widths and cell formats to match your design. If you put your column headings in first, then put in the ingredients you will get all the data in the right cells. You should be able to lock column A so it doesn't disappear off the edge of the screen as you work across the spreadsheet – check the instructions for the package you're using to find out how to do this. Next, put in the formulae. When you have got this far you should save your work on disk with a sensible name.

Now put in the data. The answers will probably appear straight away – if they don't you might have to give a command to make the spreadsheet do calculations. Sometimes the answers don't appear because the column isn't wide enough to fit them in.

You should check that the answers you're getting make sense – if they don't you've probably made a mistake in the formulae, or perhaps some of your numbers are being treated as text. When your spreadsheet is working properly, save it again with a different name.

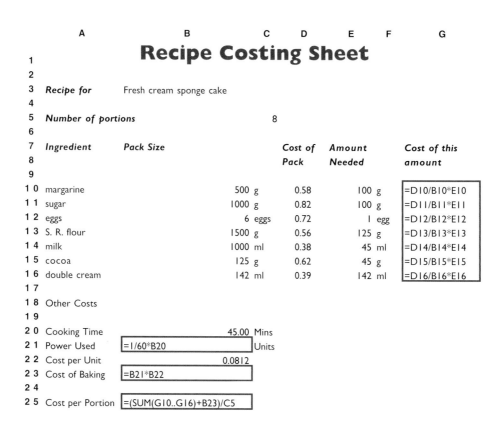

Figure 9.3 Recipe spreadsheet. Column B has had to be made wider to fit in the formula in cell B25, and column G has been expanded to fit in the formulae.

You will probably want to print out your finished spreadsheet. You can print it with the answers in and also with formulae. The recipe spreadsheets in Figures 9.3 and 9.4 show these two types of printout. In Figure 9.3 you can see that column B has had to be made wider to fit in the formula in cell B25, and column G needed to be wider to fit in the formulae in G10 to G16.

Recipe Costing Sheet

	A	B	C	D	E	F	G
1							
2							
3	Recipe for	Fresh cream sponge cake					
4							
5	Number of portions		8				
6							
7	Ingredient	Pack Size		Cost of	Amount		Cost of this
8				Pack	Needed		amount
9							
10	margarine	500 g		0.58	100 g		0.12
11	sugar	1000 g		0.82	100 g		0.08
12	eggs	6 eggs		0.72	1 egg		0.12
13	S. R. flour	1500 g		0.56	125 g		0.05
14	milk	1000 ml		0.38	45 ml		0.02
15	cocoa	125 g		0.62	45 g		0.22
16	double cream	142 ml		0.39	142 ml		0.39
17							
18	Other Costs						
19							
20	Cooking Time	45.00 Mins					
21	Power Used	0.75 Units					
22	Cost per Unit	0.0812					
23	Cost of Baking	0.06					
24							
25	Cost per Portion	0.13					

Figure 9.4 *The same spreadsheet, without the formulae.*

STEP 7: USE THE SPREADSHEET TO ANSWER THE QUESTIONS YOU STARTED WITH

▶ How would cutting the cake into smaller or bigger pieces affect the cost of a portion?

▶ How does changing the price of the ingredients affect the cost of a portion?

▶ Find out how a change in energy costs affects the cost of a portion.

In this spreadsheet some costs have a much bigger effect than others on the cost of each portion. What will have the biggest effect? What would you need to do if you decided to sell the cake and make a 25% profit?

Write down the stages you go through when you are constructing a computer model.

What checks should you carry out to ensure that a computer model is going to accurately reflect the situation or process you want it to?

Summary

- Spreadsheets are not the only way of constructing computer models.

- All models have rules.

- It is important to get these rules correct or the model won't work as you expect it to and the answers you get will be wrong.

- Even a simple model will probably have quite a lot of rules.

- If the data you use isn't accurate the model won't work as you expect and you will get misleading answers.

Suggestions for modelling work

SCIENCE

- Investigate the acceleration of a moving object.

- Investigate the effect of temperature on the rate of a chemical reaction.

- Investigate the effect of light intensity on the volume of oxygen released during photosynthesis.

TECHNOLOGY/DESIGN TECHNOLOGY

- Investigate the costs of project work, varying the materials used.

ECONOMICS/BUSINESS STUDIES

- Create a model based on rules of supply and demand and look at the effects that changing prices will have.

SKILLS

When you have completed the work in this chapter you should be able to:

- Identify a situation or process you could model using a spreadsheet.

- Decide what questions you could answer.

- Work out the data you would need to get these answers.

- Work out the rules for your model.
- Design and set up your spreadsheet model.
- Use your spreadsheet to answer the questions you started with.

Questions

I 'Ewe and Wool' is a small business that makes woollen items of clothing. The owner has created a spreadsheet to help him calculate the cost of making each item. The spreadsheet display is given below.

	A	B	C	D	E	F	G	H
I	**TYPE**	**COST OF WOOL**	**TIME TAKEN TO MAKE I**	**PAY PER HOUR**	**TOTAL PAY FOR I**	**TOTAL COST**		
2		*(£)*	*(h)*	*(£)*	*(£)*	*(£)*		
3	Cardigan	5.00	3	3.00	9.00	14.00		
4	Sweater	5.00	2	2.50	5.00	10.00		
5	Gloves	1.50	2	3.00	6.00	7.50		
6	Scarf	3.00	1	2.00	2.00	5.00		
7	Hat	2.00	1	2.00	2.00	4.00		
8								
9								

a How is the total pay calculated by the spreadsheet?

A Cost of wool × pay per hour
B Cost of wool × time taken to make one
C Time taken to make one × total cost for one
D Time taken to make one × pay per hour

b Which other values does the spreadsheet work out for you?

c The workers who knit the sweaters are unhappy about their pay and the owner decides to increase their pay per hour to £2.75. He needs to see the effect on the total cost for one item. Which cell or box on the spreadsheet would he have to change?

d The design for the cardigan changes and it will now take longer to make one.

(i)   Which cell or box would have to change?
(ii) Which other cells would change as a result?

e To give a clearer view of production the owner decides that weekly figures are needed and you are asked to extend the spreadsheet to take these into account.

You will need to add columns for:

Number made each week
Weekly cost (£)

You will also have to make the spreadsheet calculate the total weekly cost.

Explain how you would create these columns and how they are related to each other and to the rest of the spreadsheet.

NEAB specimen material

2 A milkman orders milk of various types (full cream, skimmed, semi-skimmed) and other produce from a dairy and delivers it to many customers. The milkman wants to use a spreadsheet to manage the ordering and billing system for his daily deliveries to customers' homes.

    a Use a grid to show the main elements of a suitable spread sheet. Indicate the formulae that would allow you to show each customer's weekly bill and the total weekly ordering requirements for each type of product to be ordered from the dairy.

    b The milkman will need some documentation as a reminder of how to use the system and what to do if something goes wrong. List four major aspects that should be contained in a user's manual for the system and explain why each is needed.

NEAB specimen material

3 You can use spreadsheet software to make a computer model.

    a Give an example of an investigation that you would use a spreadsheet package for to make a computer model.

    b Describe how you would set up the model on the spreadsheet.

    c Explain why you would use the computer model instead of creating the real thing.

MEG sample material

4 A local council wants to know if it should redesign a road junction. It has three options:

leave the junction as it is
put in a set of traffic lights, or
construct a roundabout.

    a Explain why a computer model could be useful to the council

    b What data would be required for the model?

    c Describe how the council could collect each item of data

SEG specimen paper   **d** What other variables might be used in the model?

CHAPTER

10 Simulation Software

Modelling using spreadsheets has many limitations – it can't respond quickly to rapidly changing inputs and its output is limited to a table of numbers containing the answer, or a graph or a chart. To simulate situations realistically the model needs to respond rapidly to inputs and the output might include changing graphics, and possibly also movement and sound. The computer program used to set up this kind of model is much more complex than a spreadsheet.

■ *Flight simulators*

A flight simulator doesn't look much like a plane!

What the inside of a flight simulator looks like.

A full-scale flight simulator of the type used to train pilots (you can see one of these in the photographs) provides a graphics display of what is visible from the plane. The 'plane' the pilot sits in is moved by motors and the dials and displays showing the position and condition of the 'plane' are updated by the computer in response to the actions the trainee pilot takes to adjust the controls. Sensors detect the pilot's adjustments and this input data is used to control the graphics display, the system that moves the 'cabin' and the readouts on the control panel. The conditions of 'flight' and 'landing' can be changed for different circumstances – for example different airports and different weather conditions – so the pilot can learn to fly without any danger.

The whole system is very complex but gives a quite realistic effect. The system collects data every time the **simulation** is run and can produce printouts to show exactly what the pilot did at each stage in the 'flight'. Even though the computer program controlling the simulator is very complex, this kind of model, like the simpler spreadsheet model, still relies on rules built into the program – the rules in a simulator are just a lot more complex than spreadsheet formulae. The simulator also produces a **real-time response** – the output is adjusted in immediate response to the input data.

A training system like this is much safer to use than learning in a real plane. It can be used to simulate emergency situations (such as engine failure or fire) and give the pilot practice in handling a dangerous situation which *might* never occur but which would require a correct and rapid response if it did happen.

■ *Other simulations*

C ar designers use simulators to test the aerodynamic effects of changes in the shape of cars. The car's shape is designed on computer using a CAD package, and the output is a mathematical description of the shape. The effects of this shape on the flow of air over it are worked out by the simulation program rather than by actually building a car body and putting it in a wind tunnel. This saves time and money and lets the designers work out how relatively small changes in the shape will affect the air flow by repeating tests – the shape can be changed and the test repeated until the designers are happy with the results.

A real wind tunnel.

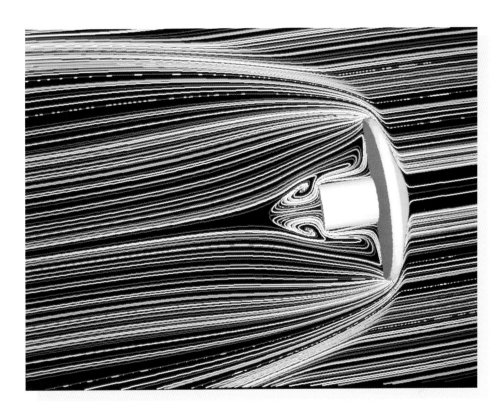

A simulation of a wind tunnel.

Can you think of any other situations where simulators are used?

Limitations of simulators

Whatever type of simulation or model is used it is very important to remember that the simulation is *not* the real world. A simulator can't *prove* what will actually happen – the model may be wrong in some way.

▶ Even a fairly simple model can have quite a lot of rules – if one of these is not always true then the results will be wrong for some situations.

▶ Variables that can affect the outcome might not have been taken into account in constructing the model.

▶ Many processes and situations can be influenced by random events like fire and bad weather conditions, so when we construct a model we must try to work out what could have an effect – even if it's unlikely.

▶ The data used in constructing the model is very important – if we put in wrong data values then the answers we get will be wrong.

Q

Why is a spreadsheet model no good for a realistic simulation like a flight simulator?

What are the benefits of using a flight simulator rather than using a real plane? Are there any disadvantages?

The quality of a simulation depends on a number of factors – what are they?

Summary

- Programs that produce realistic simulations are more complex than spreadsheet models.

- The simulation system often includes input from sensors of some kind.

- Outputs often include graphics and may include control signals to motors designed to bring about movement.

- In systems of this type, data is often collected to be analysed later.

- No matter how complex a simulation is, it is not reality and is only as good as the rules it's based on.

Questions

1 Explain why a simulator might be used for the following:

   a Training pilots
   b Investigating the effect of a river barrage scheme
   c Trying out safety systems in a new power station design
   d Designing a better shape for the body of a car

2 A flight simulator is developed as a computer game. Why would certain aspects of the control of the aircraft be omitted from the simulation?

MEG sample material

11 Measurement and Control

■ *What is control?*

Control is making things work as you want them to. A computer program can control movement. It can control the movement of a robot connected to it, opening of doors in a high security area or the movement of a screen image. If the device it is controlling is outside the computer, rather than an image on screen, then it will be connected to the computer through an **interface unit** that converts the data from the computer into signals which operate the device.

CONTROLLING AN IMAGE ON SCREEN

Let's start by thinking about how the computer controls a screen image. The computer can't move something on the screen by itself – it needs instructions telling it what to do. These instructions have to be given to the computer in a **programming language**. One language that is often used for control programs is called **LOGO**. Using instructions in LOGO a computer can be used to control a symbol called a 'turtle' on the screen, or a robot turtle on the floor (like the one in the photograph). LOGO has commands to make the turtle go forwards, backwards, left, right, stop and lift a pen up or put the pen down. A robot turtle has a real pen to draw shapes on sheets of paper on the floor – a screen 'turtle' draws a line on the screen as it moves. 'Pendown' makes the turtle draw, 'penup' stops it drawing. The 'home' instruction sends the turtle to the middle of the screen, pointing upwards.

You can use the turtle to draw pictures on the screen and to help you learn about control programs.

A robot turtle .

Most of the instructions in LOGO include a number.

> FORWARD 50 *tells the computer to move the robot forward 50 'turtle steps'.*
> LEFT 90 *tells the computer to turn the robot left through 90°.*

You can type the instructions in one at a time and the computer will carry out each instruction and wait for the next. This method will work, but you can't save your work and if you need to start again you'll have to start from the beginning. A much better method is to put the instructions together to make a program. A **program** is a series of instructions in the correct order that make the computer carry out a particular task.

LOGO programs are made up of procedures. A **procedure** is a group of instructions, with a name. In Figure 11.1 you can see a program to make the screen turtle draw a simple shape.

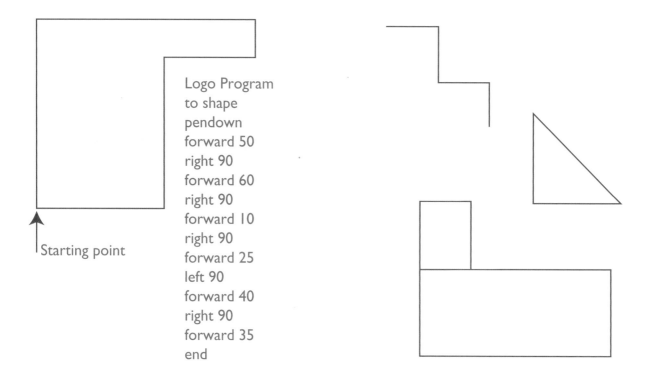

Starting point

Logo Program
to shape
pendown
forward 50
right 90
forward 60
right 90
forward 10
right 90
forward 25
left 90
forward 40
right 90
forward 35
end

Figure 11.1 *The program to make a robot turtle draw a shape.*

Figure 11.2 *Shapes to draw using LOGO.*

Look at the shapes in Figure 11.2 and try writing a LOGO program to draw them. You can use these instructions:

> *forward*
> *right*
> *left*
> *back*
> *penup*
> *pendown*

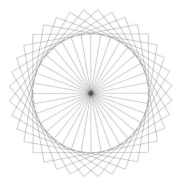

Figure 11.3 *A rather complicated looking picture, that is really prepared only using squares of the same size.*

Figure 11.4 *Different sized squares can be drawn on the same picture if you use the right procedure.*

Don't forget, if you want the computer to move the turtle you must tell it how far you want it to go. If you are telling the computer to turn the turtle you have to let it know how many degrees to turn through.

When we want to produce more complex movement or shapes, we often need to repeat the same instructions several times. LOGO gives us an easy way to do this – a repeating **loop** in the program. For example, to make a square with sides 40 'turtle steps' long, you can use this procedure:

> *to square*
> *repeat 4 [forward 40 right 90]*
> *end*

(The computer will repeat the instructions in the square brackets four times). Once you have typed in the procedure you can use the name 'square' as an instruction to draw as many squares as you want.

Figure 11.3 is a picture made entirely of squares all the same size. These squares were drawn using the instructions in this procedure:

> *to flower*
> *repeat 36 [square left 10]*
> *end*

This time there are two instructions in the brackets, which are repeated 36 times.

We don't always want to make a picture of shapes that are all the same size. If we alter the procedure called square we can allow for this. The new version is:

> *to square :side*
> *repeat 4 [forward: side right 90]*
> *end*

All you need to do to make squares of whatever size you want, in whatever position, is to write a new procedure to move the turtle to the starting point you want for each square, and provide the side length for the square procedure (this was done to give the picture in Figure 11.4).

The flower patterns in Figure 11.5 were drawn using this procedure, which we called 'pattern':

> *to pattern*
> *home*
> *pen up*
> *back 100*
> *pen down*
> *repeat 36 [square 40 left 10]*
> *pen up*
> *left 10*
> *forward 120*
> *pen down*
> *repeat 36 [square 30 left 10]*

pen up
left 10
back 40
right 90
forward 70
left 90
pen down
repeat 36 [square 20 left 10]
pen up
left 100
forward 140
right 90
pen down
repeat 36 [square 20 left 10]
end

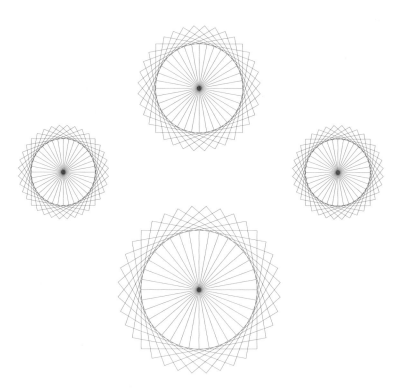

Figure 11.5 *A pattern of four flower shapes drawn using LOGO.*

Now, when we type 'pattern', the computer moves the turtle and draws a flower pattern. The movements given to the computer must be exact or we won't get proper flower shapes in the pattern we want. Read the instructions carefully and work out how the turtle is moving.

Now write some LOGO programs of your own to make repeating patterns.

Q

What is the triangular screen image used with programs like LOGO often called?

Explain what is meant by

Program
Procedure
Interface unit

Using the computer to measure changes

Computers can be used to measure changes in conditions such as temperature and amount of light (you might want to record changes in weather conditions outside your school, for example). Suitable sensors have to be attached to the computer system for it to be able to make these measurements. The sensors are attached through an interface unit or **buffer box**. A buffer box has sockets to plug in the sensors, and converts the continuously varying (**analogue**) signal from the sensor into a **digital** signal which the computer can use.

Sensors

Different kinds of sensors can be used to detect different things – like heat, light, touch (pressure) and infrared.

Before the readings from the sensors can be used, you must **calibrate** the sensor by matching particular sensor readings with known values in the units required. Once two readings have been matched the computer can calculate all the rest. For example, if you put a heat sensor in ice at 0°C and store this reading, then put it in boiling water at 100°C and store this reading, the computer will be able to work out the temperature for all the other readings between 0°C and 100°C.

Choosing the right sensor

You must be very careful to choose the right sensor for what you are going to measure. Different heat sensors work over different ranges of temperature and provide different levels of accuracy. You wouldn't use the same sensor to detect small changes in room temperature and to detect temperature changes in a central heating boiler, though you would find both kinds in a central heating control system in your home or at school.

When you are designing a system that will use sensors you need to consider these factors:

▶ What you are measuring

A computer can be used to interface with sensors.

▶ What range of values you expect to read.

▶ How the sensors will be positioned.

▶ How they will be protected – if you want to use a sensor to measure air temperature you will have to protect it from direct sunlight or you won't get an accurate reading (why?).

Using data from sensors

The computer program can use the data collected from sensors to make the decisions needed to control a device accurately. For example, the data from sensors on the arm of a robot can be used to control the movement of the robot properly. Using data from sensors to control output signals like this is called **feedback**.

Sensors on the claws of a robot's 'hand' can detect the pressure which builds up as it grips an object and the computer can be programmed to switch off the claw motor when the pressure is just strong enough to grip the object but not so strong that the object gets crushed. The robot in the photograph seems to have got it just right!

Sensors are sometimes just used to collect data for use later, and the data collected is stored in files on disk. This is called **data-logging**. The computer can be programmed to store data over a certain time and the time interval between each measurement, called the **sampling interval**, can also be set.

MELTING ICE

If we want to investigate the way temperature changes as ice melts we can use a heat sensor calibrated so that the computer gives readings in °C. The sensor doesn't need to operate over a very wide range of temperatures but it *does* have to be able to detect very small temperature changes. The sensor we choose will need to be mounted in a waterproof casing so that when it is placed in the melting ice it isn't damaged by the water.

Once the apparatus is set up (as shown in the photograph), with the sensor surrounded by crushed ice in the beaker, we need to collect our data. At this stage we don't know exactly what will happen to the temperature or how long it will take to finish the experiment. We can start by collecting data over a period of about an hour and can collect data every 30 seconds or every minute (if we collect data more often than this we will use up a lot of disk space). If, during this first investigation, we find that the changes between each reading are very large, then we can stop the experiment and try again with a shorter sampling interval. If we used sampling intervals of 5 minutes we might not have enough data to be sure that no more changes had happened at the point where all the ice had melted.

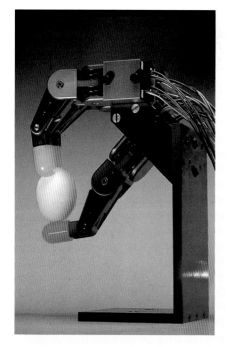

This robot's hand has to be very carefully controlled to be able to hold this egg without breaking it.

Experimental set-up for sensing the temperature in melting ice.

Once we have collected the data we can use it to plot graphs or the data can be transferred into a spreadsheet package to be used in calculations. Figure 11.6 is a graph produced from data collected in an experiment like this.

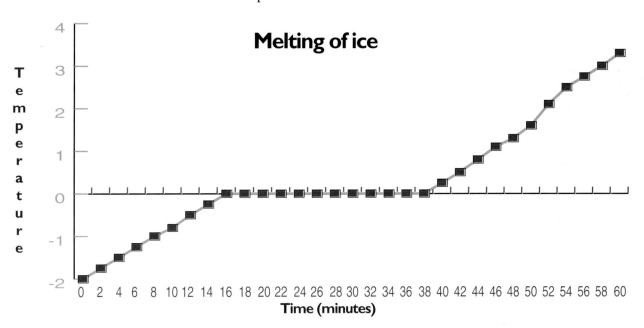

Figure 11.6 *Graph that has been produced from data collected in an experiment.*

We could keep the computer and the sensor close together in this experiment but this isn't possible for some data-logging applications. For example, when weather forecasters collect data about weather conditions in remote areas the sensors have to transmit the data to the computer over long distances, which often involves satellite systems.

A weather balloon sends its data back to the ground by telemetry.

Data about atmospheric conditions can be collected by attaching the sensing equipment to a weather balloon (you can see one in the photograph) which rises through the air. As it does so it transmits data about the altitude and weather conditions back to the computer on the ground. This sort of data transmission is called **telemetry**.

Constructing a device that responds to data from sensors

To learn about feedback and how devices can be made to respond to data collected by sensors you can make a model. Your model will have devices for the computer to control, and sensors to collect data.

For safety and legal reasons you must not try to control mains-powered equipment. Use batteries or a low-voltage power supply.

A MODEL GREENHOUSE CONTROL SYSTEM

In this section we are going to build a model of a greenhouse. The computer must keep the temperature above 18°C, turn the light on when it gets dark, turn the heater off if the temperature gets above 22°C and turn the light off when there is normal daylight in the greenhouse.

The model greenhouse control system is an example of the use of feedback – data from a sensor is used to control a device which can alter the conditions the sensor detects. Figure 11.7 shows how feedback works in this system.

Q

Name four different kinds of things which sensors can detect

Describe the process of calibration

List three details you need to consider when you are designing a system that will use sensors

What is meant by data-logging?

Give an example of data-logging where the computer and sensor(s) are close together

Give an example of data-logging in which the data from the sensor(s) would have to be transmitted over long distances

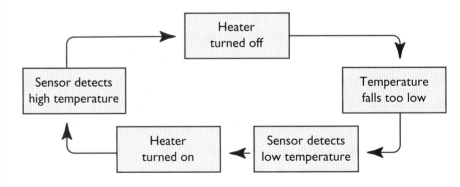

Figure 11.7 *How feedback works in a greenhouse control system.*

STEP 1: DESIGN THE GREENHOUSE MODEL

It needs to be transparent so light can get in. You will need room for the sensors, the light and the heater. You will probably want to build your model, but you don't need to put plants inside. Remember, this is just a model so it can be quite small and simple – a big clear jar would probably do.

STEP 2: DECIDE ON THE SENSORS YOU WILL USE AND WHERE YOU NEED TO PLACE THEM

You need to think about the range of temperatures that will probably be measured and choose the right kind of heat sensor. You will also need a light sensor that can operate over a very wide range of light conditions, from very dark to bright sunlight.

STEP 3: DECIDE ON WHAT DEVICES YOU WILL NEED TO KEEP THE GREENHOUSE CONDITIONS JUST RIGHT

In this model you need to control a light and a heater. The model isn't very big so choose ones with low power ratings.

STEP 4: PUT THE SENSORS AND DEVICES IN PLACE AND CONNECT THEM TO THE COMPUTER THROUGH THE INTERFACE UNIT

Be very careful when you're placing the sensors. Don't get them too close to the devices they work with or you won't get good results. If the heat sensor is directly above the heater then the sensor will get warm before the rest of your model greenhouse warms up. Why shouldn't you let light from your light bulb hit the light sensor?

You could use a kit like this to build your model greenhouse

STEP 5: DESIGN AND WRITE A PROGRAM TO READ THE SENSOR DATA AND TURN THE DEVICES ON AND OFF AS NEEDED

You must be careful about how far you let the temperature change before switching the heater on or off. If you use very narrow temperature limits you'll end up switching the heater on and off very frequently – maybe several times a second – and this level of control isn't necessary in a greenhouse. You also need to program the computer to turn the light on when it gets dark and off when it gets light, but you don't want it flashing on and off. In a real greenhouse flashing lights would disturb the people working with the plants.

Designing a program needs special care. You have to decide what the program must be able to do and produce a plan (called an **algorithm**) to show how you will make the program do this, stage by stage. The best way to prepare your design is to work out the main stages first then write down the steps needed to make each stage happen. Remember – you're designing a program for the computer, not actions for you to carry out.

Main stages

These are the main stages you'll need to think about:

1   Calibrate sensors
2   Set allowed ranges for light and temperature
3   Set interval for checking sensors
4   Check sensors and if necessary adjust heater and light (repeat this stage continuously).

Now, looking at each stage in more detail, let's decide what steps each stage requires.

Stage 1

- Read heat sensor at known temperature 1

- Store temperature 1

- Read heat sensor at known temperature 2

- Store temperature 2

- Calibrate heat sensor

- Read light sensor in bright daylight

- Store light intensity 1

- Read light sensor in dark

- Store light intensity 2

- Calibrate light sensor.

Stage 2

- Store maximum temperature allowed
- Store minimum temperature allowed
- Store maximum light allowed
- Store minimum light allowed.

Stage 3

- Store time interval to use between each set of sensor readings.

Stage 4

Repeat these steps until the computer is switched off:

- Read heat sensor
- If temperature is below the minimum allowed then turn heater on
- If temperature is above the maximum allowed then turn heater off
- If light is less than the minimum allowed then turn light on
- If light is more than or equal to the minimum allowed then turn light off
- Wait for time interval.

You can easily convert this plan into a computer program in a suitable language like Control LOGO or BASIC.

STEP 6: TEST YOUR GREENHOUSE CONTROL SYSTEM TO CHECK THAT IT WORKS

You need to check that the light goes on when it is dark. Cover up the model or put it in a box to do this test.

Check that the temperature stays within the limits you have set. You can do this by putting a thermometer inside the model and reading the temperature frequently. You could try cooling your model down by putting it next to an open window or in a fridge.

OTHER CONTROL SYSTEMS

The greenhouse control system we've just described is just one example of using feedback. Similar systems are used to control the conditions inside large buildings or to control manufacturing processes, for example producing sheets of metal of required thickness. Can you think of any others?

Summary

- A computer is capable of controlling an external device or an image on the screen when it is programmed in an appropriate way.

- Controlling a device needs a program to tell the computer what to do.

- The instructions you give the computer must be accurate or it won't control the device as you expect it to.

- Computers can be used to collect data using sensors. This is called data-logging.

- Different sensors detect different things, over different ranges and to different degrees of accuracy.

- The intervals between reading the sensor values must be suitable for the investigation being carried out. Sometimes you need to try a few different intervals to find which works best.

- The time over which data is collected must be suitable for the investigation being carried out.

- Data can be collected using sensors a long way from the computer.

- The data collected can be saved on disk for analysis in other software packages.

- When you design a system in which a device responds to data that has been collected it is important to think about the type of sensor, where it is placed, what protection it needs and the program that collects the data and controls the device.

■ *Suggestions for control and measurement work*

- Write programs in LOGO to draw shapes or control a turtle.

- Set up a computer system to compare the variation in temperature in a room and the variation in the temperature outside, saving the data so you can analyse it later.

INVESTIGATIONS

Using a computer, interface unit and software,

- investigate the movement of a trolley along a ramp

- measure temperature changes during a chemical reaction
- measure the heat given off by decomposing leaves
- construct a model of a burglar alarm system
- construct a model of a car park barrier
- use data from sensors to monitor the temperature of a fish tank and sound an alarm if it gets too hot or too cold.

Start here

Figure 11.8 A sign that can be painted by the robot arm.

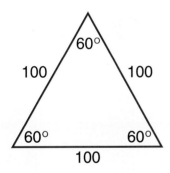

Figure 11.9 Triangle to be drawn by the turtle (1cm=10 turtle steps).

MEG sample material

Questions

1 A computer can control a robot painting arm using these commands:

UP n cm

DOWN n cm

LEFT n°

RIGHT n °

STOP

PAINT – turns on paint

NOPAINT – turns off paint

The arm is painting the sign in the picture left. Write a set of instructions to do this.

2 List three different types of sensor which can be used to detect changing environmental conditions.

3 Describe a situation in which data could be collected by sensors not directly connected to the computer. Why would this be best?

4 When data is collected it is often stored on disk. What is this type of data collection called?

5 Suggest a method of collecting data about movement of people along a corridor using sensors and storing the data on disk.

6 A floor turtle contains a pen and faces east. The turtle follows these instructions:

PEN UP	**Lift the pen off the floor**
PEN DOWN	**Place the tip of the pen on the floor**
FORWARD n	**Move n steps forward**
BACKWARD n	**Move n steps backward**
LEFT b	**Turn left b degrees**
RIGHT b	**Turn right b degrees**

Write instructions for the turtle to draw the triangle opposite.

Questions cont'd

7 A microprocessor is being used to control the temperature of a liquid in a science experiment. The system should keep the liquid at 25°C.

  a Complete this method of doing the task by filling in the blank spaces.

  1. Repeat
  2. Read the temperature
  3. If the temperature is   25°C then make sure the heater is on   , else make sure   .
  4. Until the experiment is finished

  b How would the microprocessor find out the temperature of the liquid?

MEG sample material

8 An automatic weather station on the roof of a house is connected to a home computer and suitable software.

  a Describe how such an information system might be used to collect and store weather data.
  b Give two reasons why it may be better to use a computer to help record the weather than use a manual record.
  c Two weather stations are available:
  A one that needs to be connected to the computer at all times.
  B one that collects the data inside the station for transmission at a later date.
  Discuss the relative merits of these two systems.

MEG sample material

9 A data-logger has been set up to monitor the growth of seedlings in a greenhouse. It measures the plants' intake of carbon dioxide (CO_2). A sensor measures the concentration of CO_2 in the air and as the seedlings grow they use up more CO_2 and the concentration in the air drops.

   Explain how you could modify the equipment either to detect when the seeds' leaves begin to unfurl, or adjust the concentration of CO_2 so that it is always at the correct level for maximum growth of the seedlings. A cylinder of CO_2 is available in the greenhouse.

MEG sample material

10 Tilda Shower is a geography teacher. Tilda wants the school weather station to provide her class with very detailed weather data over a period of a week.

   The instructions below are part of a computer program which, every 30 minutes, stores the temperature that the weather station detects.

WAIT 30

DETECT TEMP

STORE TEMP

  a Tilda now wants the temperature to be stored every 15 minutes. Show how one of the instructions will have to be changed.

Questions cont'd

b (i) Explain why these instructions by themselves would not keep on storing the temperature.
(ii) Show the extra instructions that would be needed so that the computer will store the temperature 'forever'.
(You may invent your own instructions.)

c 50°C is very hot
−50°C is very cold
Sometimes the weather station does not work properly so silly values of temperature are stored.
Explain how the program could be improved to prevent the computer storing silly values for temperature.

d Tilda wants the rainfall data to be recorded every hour for a whole year. She also wants the results to be printed in the form of a booklet.
(i) Describe how this amount of data could have been collected without the aid of a computer.
(ii) Explain why, in a school, it would not be practicable to collect this amount of data without a computer.
(iii) State one advantage to Tilda's pupils of having this amount of data.

ULEAC specimen material

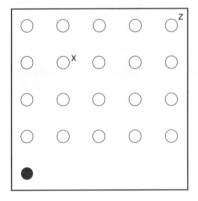

Figure 11.10

SEG specimen paper

11 A robot is used to retrieve fuel rods from a nuclear reactor. To get the rod labelled 'X', the following instructions could be given:

FORWARD 3

TURN RIGHT

FORWARD 1

TAKE

a Write sensible instructions to get this rod placed into position Z and bring the robot back to its starting place.

b The robot has an instruction (INPUT var) that allows numbers to be in put into variables, which can then be used instead of the numbers indicated above. Write a programme so that it will allow any rod to be retrieved. Make sure you clearly identify the use of your variables.

c Why should a robot be used for this job?

12 A car park entrance is controlled by a microprocessor. When a car approaches the barrier a ticket is produced, which the driver takes. The barrier then opens, and the lights change from red to green. When the car has passed through, the light changes to red and the barrier comes down.

a Describe a suitable sensor for detecting the approaching car.

b List the steps involved in carrying out this process, using suitable instructions.

SEG specimen paper

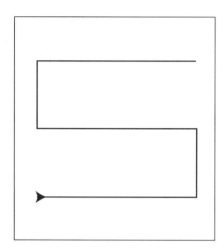

Figure 11.11 S shape.

NEAB specimen material

13 A computer can control a turtle on the screen. When the turtle moves it leaves a line on the screen. Some of the commands are:

FORWARD steps

BACK steps

RIGHT angle

LEFT angle

For example,

FORWARD 50 moves the turtle forward 50 steps in a straight line

RIGHT 45 turns the turtle 45° to the right.

Here are the commands which are needed to draw the S shape:

FORWARD 50	LEFT 50
FORWARD 50	LEFT 90
FORWARD 100	RIGHT 90
FORWARD 100	RIGHT 90
FORWARD 100	

The turtle starts from the position shown in the diagram. Arrange these commands in the right order to draw the S shape.

14 A computer is used to control a robot that is moving and stacking boxes in a warehouse. It uses the same commands that were used to control the turtle and has two extra commands to raise and lower its forks. These are:

UP steps

DOWN steps

It is found dropping the boxes in the wrong place.

a Give three reasons why this could be happening

b Following a nasty accident the robot has had to be adapted to stop if it meets and unexpected obstacle in its path. What changes would need to be made to the robot design?

NEAB specimen material

15 The table shows a number of different situations. Fill in the boxes to show the time intervals between logging and the overall period of logging.

Questions cont'd

SITUATION	SENSOR	TIME INTERVAL	PERIOD OF LOGGING
Collecting data on seasonal temperature variations for weather records	Heat		
Collecting data about the temperature change which takes place when ice is added to a beaker of water	Heat		

NEAB specimen material

16 The greenhouse shown in the diagram must be kept at a temperature between 23°C and 27°C throughout the year. It has been decided to use a computer-controlled system. Produce an outline design for the system required.

Figure 11.12 Greenhouse

12 Evaluating Software Packages

Y ou'll often find that you need to choose from several software packages of the same type when you're solving a particular IT problem – you might have two or three different spreadsheet packages available, more than one database package, and two or three different word processing packages.

A selection of word processing packages.

Choosing which *kind* of package you need to use is nearly always quite straightforward, but deciding *which* package of that type will do the job best is not quite so easy.

You can't make reasoned decisions unless you **evaluate** each of the packages available. Evaluating a package means finding out how well it does the kind of job you want it to do. You can't do this without having a list of tasks the package must carry out.

For example, if you want to produce a report of a science experiment you might need to use a package which can:

▶ handle ordinary text

▶ handle special characters, for example letters from the Greek alphabet (α, β, γ)

- produce subscripts, for example the number 2 in the formula H_2O
- produce superscripts – for example the 3 in cm^3
- produce neat tables with numbers and headings lined up properly
- import charts from a spreadsheet
- import drawings from a drawing package
- allow large files for long reports
- number the pages
- be easy to use with help available on screen when needed.

You will need to find out if the word-processing package can do these things, and also how easily it does them.

To carry out an evaluation, make a complete list of everything you need the package to do. Put these in order of importance because sometimes you will have to settle for the best package available when none of them do everything you would like. Remember, how easy the package is to use is very important, especially if you are producing a system to be used by other, inexperienced users.

Once your list is complete, work through all the tasks for one package, and give the package a score for each item (you might give 5 points if it does the job well, 4 if there are one or two minor difficulties, 3 if it is quite hard to learn to carry out a task, 2 if the task takes far too long and is difficult to carry out, 1 if it can only be done with extreme difficulty, so that you would probably avoid doing it at all and 0 if it doesn't do the task at all). Be consistent in your scoring. When you have done this for all your packages you will be able to make a reasoned judgement about which package is best.

If you're asked to recommend a package to someone else, you shouldn't just give them your scores because they might not mean much to someone else. You should produce an evaluation report, explaining what tasks you have tried, what you have found out, and include some printouts of what the packages can do. At the end of your report you should describe the strengths and weaknesses you have found and make your recommendation.

Questions

I A local council is planning to build a new road. They will use information technology at many stages of the planning. Some of the systems available to them are:

CAD (computer aided design)
Data-logging
Database
DTP (desktop publishing)
Spreadsheet
Word-processing

Questions cont'd

Choose from this list the most sensible system for each job below. Write your answer against each job (use each item once only).

COUNTING CARS USING EXISTING ROADS

MAKING AN INFORMATION BOOKLET

ANALYSING A QUESTIONNAIRE

DESIGNING A BRIDGE

ESTIMATING THE COSTS

WRITING TO CONTRACTORS

SEG specimen paper

13 Producing and Documenting Systems

If you have worked through this book you will already have designed some systems that use IT to solve specific problems. You will probably have written down something about the systems you have produced, but you probably won't have fully **documented** your systems. **Documentation** is the written material (the **document**) that explains how a system works and how to use it. Producing good, clear documentation is as important as designing a good, efficient system. If the people who want to use your system can't understand the instructions you've written then the whole system is a failure.

When you're producing a system for others to use it is vital that it works as efficiently as possible, so the user can get what they want out of it as quickly and easily as possible.

■ Producing the system specification

It is very important to find out everything that the user needs the system to do, but finding this out isn't always easy! Your user might not know much about IT so you might need to make helpful suggestions. When users describe what they want from a system, they often miss out important tasks, perhaps because they don't happen very often. You will need to talk to the people who will use your system and make notes about what they say they want the system to do. If your system is intended to replace an existing way of doing the job, you will find that watching what happens at present will help you make sure nothing gets left out. You will also need to check for any **constraints** on the system you produce – your user might need a system that works on a particular make of computer, or can only afford to pay a certain amount for the final system.

When you have collected all this information you can write a **system specification**. The system specification says what the system must be able to do. It may also:

▶ include information on the number of records or amount of data the system must be able to handle and store

▶ say how quickly the output must be produced

▶ specify the computer system to be used

▶ give a date when the system must be complete and ready for use.

The system specification needs to be quite detailed as it will be used to decide whether the final system performs as it should. A successful system meets all the requirements in the system specification.

■ Producing a school newsletter

To make the process clearer, let's look at how we would create a system to produce a school newsletter. The newsletter will be issued free to all pupils every two weeks. It is to be produced by a group of pupils and staff and duplicated in the school office.

Here is the specification for the system:

1 The system must be capable of including line drawings, photographs and text.
2 The newsletter will be printed in black on coloured paper.
3 A standard heading will be used for all issues.
4 Pages will always be divided into two columns.
5 Apart from the front page, all pages will have the same layout.
6 Articles and news items will be collected from pupils and staff and most will be hand-written.
7 The newsletter must be put together within two days of collecting all the news items.
8 It must be possible to alter what is on the pages after the first copy is printed and before all the copies are duplicated.
9 The system must not cost too much.

■ Designing the system

Once you've produced your specification you can work out how data will move through the system.

Always start by thinking about what you want to come out of the system (you should do this whenever you're designing anything). From there you can work out what you need to put in and link the two together by describing the **processing stages** involved in producing the outputs.

Remember, you are designing the *whole* system so you will need to think about human processing as well as computer processing and the flow of data.

As you begin to work out the kind of processing the computer has to do you will need to make decisions about the kind of package or packages you will use. You should base your decisions on what type of package can do the job best. *Do* consider all possible approaches – the first one you think of might not be the best. It is certainly *not* a good idea to decide on the package first and then try to make the system design fit what this package can do.

For some systems you might need to use more than one software package – or you might choose an **integrated package** to allow you to move data easily between your word processor, your spreadsheet and your database. Don't be tempted to add extra parts to the system just to use more sections of the integrated package – stick to the system specification. For our newsletter system we will use a word processor to prepare text files, a scanner and scanning software to prepare picture files and DTP software to put the pages together.

You need to be very clear about how data will move through your system. You could describe this in writing or show it as a diagram like the one in Figure 13.1. This kind of diagram is called a **system flowchart**.

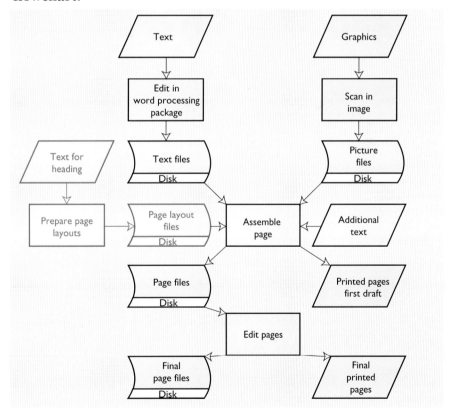

Figure 13.1 *Here is an example of a system flowchart, showing how data flows through the system. This figure shows the system used for producing the school newsletter. The sections shown in red will only happen when the system is set up, but the sections in black will happen every time the newsletter is produced.*

System flowcharts use certain shapes to represent input and output, processing and files stored on disk or tape – you can see some of these in Figure 13.2.

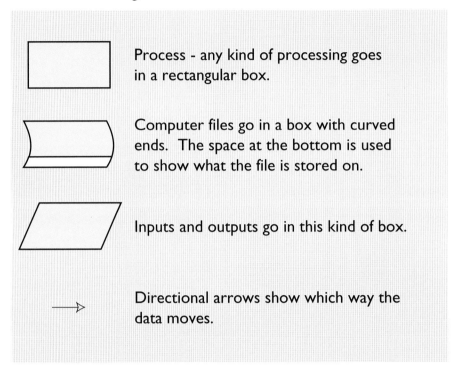

Process - any kind of processing goes in a rectangular box.

Computer files go in a box with curved ends. The space at the bottom is used to show what the file is stored on.

Inputs and outputs go in this kind of box.

Directional arrows show which way the data moves.

Figure 13.2 *Some of the symbols you will find on a system flowchart.*

You will have to identify each main task you need to complete to make your system work. (The main tasks are the ones drawn in rectangles in the system flow chart.) Make a list of the main tasks then, once you've decided on the software and worked out how everything links together, you can get on with the detailed design work for each of the main tasks.

Remember, always start with the outputs needed and work out the inputs and processing requirements. When your design is complete someone else should be able to use it as a basis for setting up the system and getting it to work.

(We have already looked at design in detail in Chapters 3, 6, 8 and 11. Look back at these if you need to refresh your memory.)

■ *Designing the tests*

Try to work out what tests you will need to test the whole system during the design stage. To test our newsletter system we will have to:

▶ prepare text files

▶ scan some pictures

▶ assemble one page of each type using the prepared outlines

▶ print each page

▶ rearrange the pages

▶ save the pages to disk

▶ print the newsletter in its final version.

We will need to try text files of different sizes, and pictures of different sizes and types.

Implementing the design

Implementing is setting up the system and making it work as it should. This is done using the software packages you have chosen – you will find this easiest if you tackle it one main task at a time. Always start with the essential tasks needed for the system (pretty introduction screens are not essential!) and as you complete each main task, test it to check that it works and that it matches the original specification.

The newsletter system is fairly simple but you will need to set up a **document template** for the word processor, so that you don't end up with different news items in different fonts and with different margins. You will also need to set up the scanner and scanning software for the kind of pictures you will be given – you might find that the scanner settings have to be different for different kinds of picture. Make a note of the settings that work best so you can put instructions in the **user guide** when you write it. You might be able to set up the software so that it always saves the picture files in the format you need.

The biggest task is creating the page layout files.

▶ You will have to put in the fixed heading on the layout for the first page.

▶ You will also have to set up the columns and fonts to be used on this page.

▶ You must then save this page.

▶ You must also create the layout file for the other pages in the same way.

Testing the system

Testing must use three kinds of data (remember this from the chapter on databases?):

Typical data – to make sure it is handled as it ought to be. For the newsletter this will consist of short text files and small picture files.

Data on boundaries – to make sure the boundaries of the system are set correctly. For the newsletter this will consist of files too big to fit in a column and files too big to fit on a page.

Data which is wrong – to make sure **error trapping** works properly. For the newsletter this will consist of picture files in the wrong file format and text files which include unwanted fonts and the wrong margins.

You will need to prepare a **testing plan** to make sure that all the parts of your system are tested fully – without a plan you could miss out important aspects of testing. Testing the newsletter system is straightforward but other systems are more difficult to test fully. Table 13.1 shows how to plan for testing a database system.

TEST NO.	SELECTION TESTED	NATURE OF TEST	RESULT OF TEST (+ REFERENCE)
1	Data Collection	Use all sheets to collect data	*Put results and comments here as testing done.*
2	Entry of record	Valid data for all fields	*Include references to print outs*
		Invalid data	
3	Editing of record	Changes to each field existing	
4	Deletion of record	Record no. to delete non-existent record number	
5	Report production TEST ALL REPORTS THIS WAY	Selection of report by name	
6	Backup procedures	Do a backup	
	Recovery procedures	Restore a backup	
7	User documentation	Get the user to work through the User Guide	

Table 13.1

When you are testing a system you will have to put some data into it. You must choose this data carefully to be sure that it will let you carry out all the tests you need and give you useful results. Write out your test data and the reasons you have chosen it. Check that it will let you test every possible way of using the system correctly, and all the possible ways of using it wrongly.

TESTING THE WHOLE SYSTEM

In addition to testing that the tasks carried out by the computer work as they should, you will need to test the *entire* system when it has been put together to make sure that it all works properly together – this includes testing the human stages as well as the computer stages. You must prove that the system you have produced matches the system specification.

Testing must take into account all of the original specifications for the system. For example, if your system is supposed to be easy for young children to use, then your testing plan must include a session where young children try it out. You will need to test the newsletter system by asking the team producing the newsletter to try it out.

Good testing takes time, so if you are developing a system you should allow plenty of time for the testing stage – don't expect to do all the testing in a few minutes.

Record the results of your tests carefully, and get printouts to show what happens in the tests. The best way of doing this is to draw up a table to describe each test, what it is testing, the results you expect, and the results you get.

Documenting the system

It is important to provide written information about your system (once it's working) so that other people can use it properly. This kind of written information is known as documentation. Two main types of documentation are usually provided with an IT system.

Maintenance documentation provides technical information about how the system was set up and how the parts are connected. It should include the test plans and results of the tests. It is designed to allow another competent person to look after the system and keep it up to date.

User documentation provides the person who will use your system with a set of instructions to tell them how to make the system work as it should.

When you write user documentation you will need to provide:

- Instructions for setting up the system
- Instructions, in a logical order, for normal use of the system
- Instructions for dealing with errors
- Instructions for making **copies** (backup copies) of all the data files and programs
- Instructions for recovering from a system failure – for example, if there is a power cut and some of the data files are lost.

Remember, you should test your user guide together with the system. The system won't be of any use if the users can't understand your instructions.

When you write the maintenance documentation for the newsletter system you should include:

▶ The system flowchart to show how data moves through the system

▶ Full details of how the word processing template document was set up, including margins, font selected and the text style

▶ Instructions on how to set up the scanning software (including scanner settings and file formats to be used to save picture files)

▶ The design sheets for the page layouts with details of the heading text, its font, size and style

▶ Details of the fonts, sizes and styles you set up for the rest of the text on the page

▶ A list of the file formats the package can accept and what it has been set up to expect.

All of this information would be very useful if you, or someone else, needed to make a few changes in the future.

In the user documentation for the newsletter system you would need to provide very clear instructions for carrying out every task.

▶ You would have to start by telling the user how to load the word-processing package and the text file template, then explain how to enter and save text.

▶ For the scanner and scanning software, after telling the user how to load the software, you would have to explain how to set the scanner for different kinds of picture and how to work the scanner and its software to scan the picture. Scanned pictures usually need some editing, so you should explain how to do this. You will have to provide clear instructions about saving the picture file in the right format.

▶ For the DTP package, you would need to explain how to load the package and then the page layout files for each kind of page. You would need to provide step-by-step instructions on how to put prepared text files into the page, how to put pictures into the page and also how to rearrange the page and change the size of pictures if necessary. You should include instructions for saving the finished page and also for printing the page.

▶ You also need to tell the user how to make backup copies of the files, and explain how to use the backup disks if the original files are ever lost.

▶ Your user documentation should also include a list of the problems the user's most likely to come across, what causes them and how to fix them.

Summary

- Good systems design begins with analysing the users' requirements.

- When you know exactly what the user wants, produce a specification for the system. The specification will be the basis for checking that the system does everything it should.

- Work out ways of producing the system. Always look at alternatives and think about the advantages and disadvantages of the alternatives.

- Produce a plan to show how data will flow through your system.

- Design all the parts of the system.

- Implement the system using the packages you have selected.

- Test your system, making sure that all the parts work as they ought to. To do this you will need to construct a testing plan and select the right kind of test data.

- When you know your system is working properly, write your documentation. This usually includes maintenance documentation and a user guide.

Questions

I Write a description of each stage involved in producing an information system for someone else to use.

2 a Why is it important to produce a list of the requirements of a system?
  b What would you include in this list if you were developing a new system?
  c What uses would you make of this list?

3 a Why must testing of a system be planned carefully?
  b What are the general rules for selecting test data?
  c How would you present the results of testing a system?

14 IT in a Medical Centre

A typical Doctor's surgery.

I n this chapter we shall be looking in detail at how a Medical Centre based in a small market town in the north-east of England uses IT. It is a group practice with five Doctors and about 9,000 patients, although this has varied between 7,000 and 12,000 as the population of the town varies.

■ *Before IT*

B efore we look at the way IT was introduced into the practice, it may help us to look at the Centre before they had IT. When a patient first registered with the surgery, their personal details (name, age, sex) were taken, together with a 'medical life history'. These details were either collected from the patient themselves or from their previous Doctor. All of these details were written by hand onto record cards, which were then filed away.

After a patient was seen by a Doctor, either in the Medical Centre or at home, details of the consultation were entered onto that patients' record card and a prescription for medicine written out and given to the patient if it was needed.

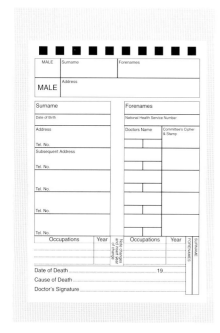

Figure 14.1 *A record card from the Medical Centre.*

Prescriptions could be written for up to a month's supply of medicine, but some patients needed to be on medication for more than one month, and were given a repeat prescription. This involved the patient calling in to the surgery, either in person or by phone, or writing a letter each month. Then the Medical Centre clerks/receptionists had to find their notes and give them to the Doctor, who would then search through the information in the notes and decide to either write out the required prescription or ask to see the patient to review their progress.

The Doctors at the Centre also carried out immunisations against particular diseases, followed up chronic illnesses and gave advice as part of their normal procedure.

Sometimes tests would have to be carried out at the Centre and sent off to a hospital for analysis, then the results were sent back by post to the Medical Centre and written on the patients' record card.

If a patient went into hospital for any reason, notes relating to this would also have to be recorded by hand on the record cards.

Introducing IT into the practice

It is worth mentioning here how the Doctors are paid by the National Health Service. The payment they receive is made up of two parts:

First, a "capitation payment" which is an amount of money for every patient on their practice's register. Secondly, "item of service payments". These are payments for particular things the doctors do. For instance, they are paid a certain amount of money for each night visit they carry out and for each immunisation they give.

These "item of service payments" usually make up about 40% of a Doctor's income so obviously it is important to count the numbers of each item carried out accurately. Keeping a check on these items is very time consuming and sometimes inaccurate if carried out by hand.

Five years ago the Doctors decided to introduce IT into the practice, in order to make all areas of the medical practice run more efficiently, and therefore provide a better service to their patients.

For a number of years previously, several pilot studies using Information Technology in medical practices had been carried out where Doctors tried out the systems and suggested improvements so, hopefully, the systems introduced now would be more useful and reliable. Government, through the Department of Health, were trying to get medical practices to invest in Information Technology equipment, so there was lots of encouragement to try the new systems out.

The main reason for change, however, was simple: to make the medical practice more efficient and provide a better service to their patients. You can see the system the Doctors chose in Figure 14.2.

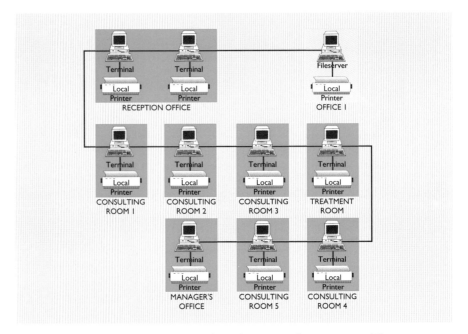

Figure 14.2 *The layout of the system chosen.*

It has nine terminals attached to the central processor. The software is easy to use and has been written specifically for medical practices. The menu in Figure 14.3 shows the major functions of the software.

MEDICAL SYSTEM

Transaction 1
IGP Training 2
System status 3
IGP Training restore 4
Prescribing Management 5
Back up to removable hard disk 6
Reporter ·· 7
Sign off ··· 8

Select :

Figure 14.3 *A screen showing major functions of the software.*

Some of these functions are used every day, others are used less often (or not at all if they are not relevant to the practice). There is a database with a record for every patient registered at the Centre.

The screen in Figure 14.4 gives the major details of a particular patient.

West Paul Ian 21yr Male 21 Broad Street

Prevention history verified   Reg exam: Offered   30/06/94 Due date

Major problems: 13/07/92   PAIN HIP
                       16/07/92   SLIPPED HIP EPIPHYSIS   ADMITTED
                       16/08/92   SCREW FIXATION BONE

Repeat medication:

1. Allergy: No record
2. Intolerance: No record
3. Contraception: No record
4. Blood pressure: No record
5. Smoking: 05/03/94 NON-SMOKER
6. Alcohol: 05/03/94 1 UNITS/WEEK
7. Recall: No record
8. * Immun/Vacc: 1 DUE 1ST TPOL
9. * Weight/Height: 77.12Kg 05/03/94 180.3cm BMI: 23.7
10. Test results: No record
11. Investigations: No record
12. Occupation: No record

SELECT
A(dd) B(ack) G(raph) N(ext) P(rint HCC) R(ecords) S(creening) <CR> Exit

Figure 14.4 A screen showing a patient's major details.

Using this system the doctor is also able to access two special database files. One is a conditions dictionary which gives information about a huge range of different diseases to help make a diagnosis. You can see a screen from this in Figure 14.5.

The other is a drugs dictionary, which is updated every two months and, as you can see from the screen in Figure 14.6, contains information on each drug – the form it comes in (tablet, injection, liquid), the dosages (or strengths) available, the drug names (both general chemical names and brand names) and any other extra notes the Doctor may find useful.

West Paul Ian 21yr Male 21 Broad Street

1 OESOPHAGUS DISEASE
2 OESOPHAGITIS
3 ACUTE OESOPHAGITIS
4 ABCESS OESOPHAGUS
5 OESOPHAGITIS PEPTIC
6 AMPULLA LOWER OESOPHAGUS
7 AMPULLA PHRENIC
8 OESOPHAGEAL REFLUX
9 GASTRO-OESOPHAGEAL REFLUX

OESOPHAGUS

Figure 14.5 A screen from the conditions dictionary.

Date	Drug Dictionary Name BUCLOSAMIDE	Form	Strength	
1		POW	10.00%	BUCLOSAMIDE/SALICYLIC ACID DIS DRUG
2		SOL	10.00%	BUCLOSAMIDE/SALICYLIC ACID DIS DRUG
3		CRE	0.2%	BUCLOSAMIDE
4		INH	100meg	BUCLOSAMIDE
5		INH	200meg	BUCLOSAMIDE
6		OIN	0.2%	BUCLOSAMIDE
7		SPR	100meg	BUCLOSAMIDE
8		INH	50meg	BUCLOSAMIDE
9		INH	100meg	BUCLOSAMIDE TURBOHALER

Figure 14.6 *A screen from the drugs dictionary.*

■ *Getting used to the system*

When the computer system was installed in the Medical Centre, all the staff were trained for three days, including the two new clerks/receptionists who were employed to help run the system, by the company they bought it from. There then followed a six-month trial period before the system could be used properly. This let the Doctors and other staff get used to the new ways of operating, as well as making sure the system worked properly.

The main task that had to be carried out was to transfer all the details from the record cards to the computer database files.

In order to get the system up and running in the shortest possible time, not all the details for each patient were transferred to the computer system at the same time. The information had to be summarised, then details were added in four distinct stages:

1   The first information to be transferred for each patient was the patient's name, date of birth, sex and address.
2   Once all of these details had been entered for each patient, data about any prescriptions the patient was receiving were added. This allowed the Centre to use the new prescription system, which we will look at later.
3   After this, details about any 'major life events' in terms of health were entered for all patients.
4   Finally, the data collected by the Doctors during their consultations with patients was put onto the database.

■ *How is the system used?*

The new computer system at the Medical Centre is used in many ways. The main use is to keep up-to-date records of every patient, which the Doctor can look up quickly and easily.

When the Doctors arrive in their consulting rooms at the Medical Centre, they are given a list of their appointments for the day which has been generated by the computer. In order to access information on the computer the Doctor has to type in a **password**, which only he or she knows, at the start of the session.

When a patient comes into the consulting room, the Doctor calls up the display for this patient by entering the patient's name (the full name does not have to be entered – if only the first few letters are typed then a list of patients in alphabetical order, starting from the letters typed is displayed and the Doctor can choose the correct one).

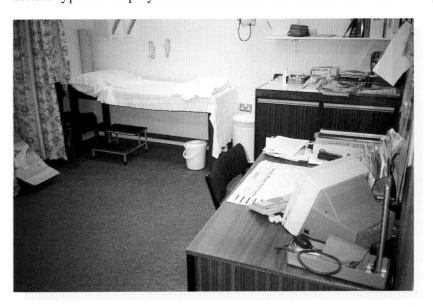

A consulting room.

The information on the screen can be seen by the Doctor and is also visible to the patient. Sometimes the Doctor feels that the patient shouldn't see some details, and she uses a 'backscreen' facility on the display to hide these details and they do not appear on the screen.

While talking with the patient, the Doctor can look up information in both the classification of drugs database and the conditions dictionary database if she needs to, although for more detailed information on a drug she would probably refer to the text book.

The Doctor can record details about the patient (perhaps their blood pressure) and, using data from several visits, can produce a graph on the computer to see if any trends are developing.

The Medical Centre still uses the old style record cards because the computer system doesn't allow the Doctors to enter detailed records and comments – it's also more time-comsuming for the Doctor to type than it is to write. But some practices have moved across to completely computer-based records.

At the end of the consultation the Doctor enters brief details about it through the keyboard of the terminal – the date, the diagnosis and any medication prescribed. This data is stored automatically, updating that patient's computer record.

If the patient needs a prescription it can be printed out in the consulting room. This prescription can contain details which, under the old manual system, were never included, for example:

▶ details of the medication for the patient to tear off and keep,

▶ a date to return to the doctor for a review of the treatment,

▶ a message about a general health issue, such as the dangers of being overweight.

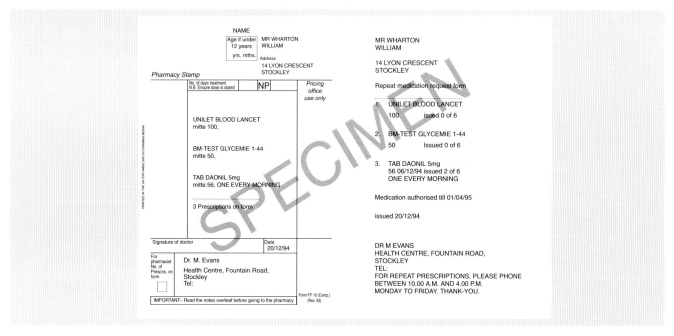

Figure 14.7 *A sample prescription with tear-off information for the patient.*

How else is the system used?

The system is used by the practice in many other ways too. Here are a few.

REPEAT PRESCRIPTIONS

When we looked at the situation before IT, there were times when a patient needed a repeat prescription. Each patient is now given a unique prescription number, which allows the clerk/receptionist to identify the patient and their prescription requirements. Each day the repeat prescription requests are processed, the prescriptions are printed and are given to the Doctor to sign. As she signs the prescriptions, the Doctor can use her terminal to check any patient details she needs. The prescription now contains the 'review' date for the treatment and if this date has been passed, the clerk/receptionist or the Doctor can ask the patient to make an appointment for a consultation.

COMMUNICATION

The introduction of IT has also made it much easier to communicate with the thousands of registered patients. For example, patients may need to be screened (checked for a particular disease) every two years. With the old system it was extremely time-consuming to check through all the patient notes regularly to check when any of them might be due for a screening. But now it is possible to search the database files very quickly for every patient whose screening is due (say) in the next month and print out letters to every one of them to make an appointment. This can be applied to many other situations – for example, children need to have vaccinations at particular ages and the database files can be interrogated to find out which ones are needed and to produce letters to the parents of children whose immunisations are due.

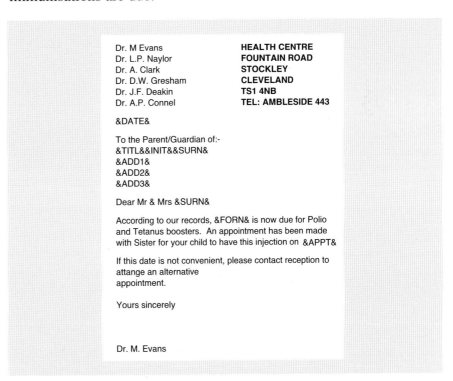

Dr. M Evans
Dr. L.P. Naylor
Dr. A. Clark
Dr. D.W. Gresham
Dr. J.F. Deakin
Dr. A.P. Connel

HEALTH CENTRE
FOUNTAIN ROAD
STOCKLEY
CLEVELAND
TS1 4NB
TEL: AMBLESIDE 443

&DATE&

To the Parent/Guardian of:-
&TITL&&INIT&&SURN&
&ADD1&
&ADD2&
&ADD3&

Dear Mr & Mrs &SURN&

According to our records, &FORN& is now due for Polio and Tetanus boosters. An appointment has been made with Sister for your child to have this injection on &APPT&

If this date is not convenient, please contact reception to attange an alternative appointment.

Yours sincerely

Dr. M. Evans

Figure 14.8 A sample immunisation reminder.

Another benefit of using a computer-based system is that a Doctor can print out an outline medical history of a patient and take it on visits to the patient's home.

'DRUG ALERTS'

Sometimes it is discovered that a particular drug has side effects, and the doctors need to find out which patients use, or have used, the drug. Before IT was introduced this would have taken a very long time and some patients might have been missed. But now the Centre can produce accurate lists of all the patients that have used this drug very quickly by searching for the drug in all the patients' records in the database file. The Doctors can also use the database to produce complex reports, perhaps linking the use of a particular drug to a particular side effect.

MEDICAL RESEARCH

One of the major benefits of having all this data stored electronically is that details of diseases as well as the characteristics of the people suffering from them, the drugs and methods used to combat these conditions and details of how successful they are, can be used to create a central database file which can be used for research purposes. For this to happen it is essential that the data sent is anonymous (the patient cannot be identified from the data) and has been verified (checked to make sure it is correct). About 800 medical practices provide this data, and the central database file now contains medical details of over two million anonymous patients. All these practices use the same file format for the data and actually send it on floppy disk.

■ *Keeping the data secure*

When you have so much personal data stored about people it is very important to make sure the data is not available to anyone who might use it to harm other people, or for their own advantage. There are strict laws and rules to prevent this including the Data Protection Act, which we shall look at in more detail in Chapter 17. In our example, the medical practice is registered as a data user with the Data Protection Registrar so it follows the regulations of the Data Protection Act.

They also have safeguards against unauthorised access to the database files in their system. All the Doctors and staff have their own password which they have to enter before they can use the system, and they also use **password hierarchies** to restrict access to data. All the terminals used by staff outside the consulting rooms are kept out of sight of 'passers by'. The system is completely contained in the building and is not connected to the telephone lines so no-one can get into the system from a computer outside.

It is also important to make sure that the data held on each patient is protected against accidental loss or damage so the Centre must make sure that it keeps copies of the data, which can be used to restore the database if it ever gets corrupted. Backup copies of the database files are taken each day for this purpose.

■ *Future developments*

O ther medical practices now use systems that have been developed from the one we have looked at here. These systems are used to store, process and retrieve all patient details, including notes and comments, and there is an automatic check built in that tells the Doctor if a drug about to be prescribed to a patient clashes with another drug they're already taking.

In the near future, improvements in the way computers in different places can communicate will allow medical practice systems to have direct links to hospitals. This will mean, for example, that a patient's test results can be sent electronically from the hospital to the practice and will automatically update a patient's records. Note that this will have implications in terms of security. The test result data transmitted from the hospital to the practice in this example will have the patient's name included and when you have electronic links like this the system is opened up to the threat of hacking (more about hacking in Chapter 17).

In the future there will probably be direct links from medical practices to the Family Health Services Authority. Doctors will be able to send details of the number of patients registered with their practice, together with the "item of service" totals for the FHSA to calculate the payments made.

15 An Urban Traffic Control System

I n this chapter we are going to look at the urban traffic control system that is in operation in the towns of Middlesbrough and Stockton-on-Tees in the county of Cleveland.

■ *What is an urban traffic control system?*

A n urban traffic control system operates the traffic lights at road junctions and pedestrian crossings and controls the flow of traffic along these roads. The system we will be looking at in this chapter has three levels for operating the traffic lights and pedestrian crossings, which work at different times of the day.

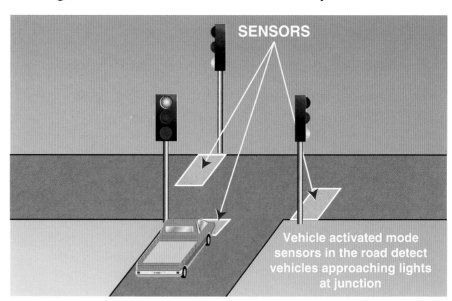

Figure 15.1 An urban traffic control system in vehicle activated mode.

'VEHICLE ACTIVATED' MODE

Traffic lights at a junction work as a set. During the evening they operate in 'vehicle activated' mode. Sensors built into the road near the junction detect when a vehicle is approaching the lights. If the lights are already on green for that vehicle then the lights won't change, but if they are on red they will change to green. (The lights for the other roads entering the junction have to be changed first.)

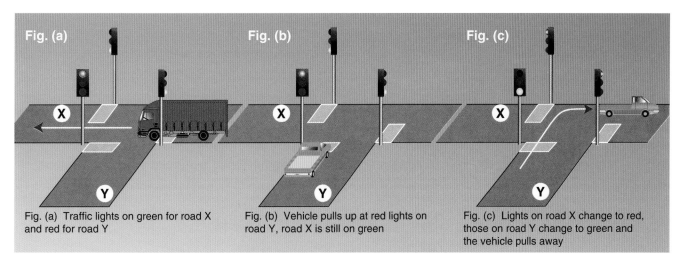

Fig. (a) Traffic lights on green for road X and red for road Y

Fig. (b) Vehicle pulls up at red lights on road Y, road X is still on green

Fig. (c) Lights on road X change to red, those on road Y change to green and the vehicle pulls away

Figure 15.2 *A vehicle-activated traffic light system.*

'FIXED TIME' MODE

If the traffic flow gets heavier, the vehicle activated mode causes problems because the lights are changed too often. The system then switches to 'fixed time' mode. At each junction, a microprocessor contains a number of different plans to control the timing of the sequence of lights. The particular plan used depends upon the time of day. The fixed time plans determine how long each part of the cycle of lights for each traffic light at the junction will last.

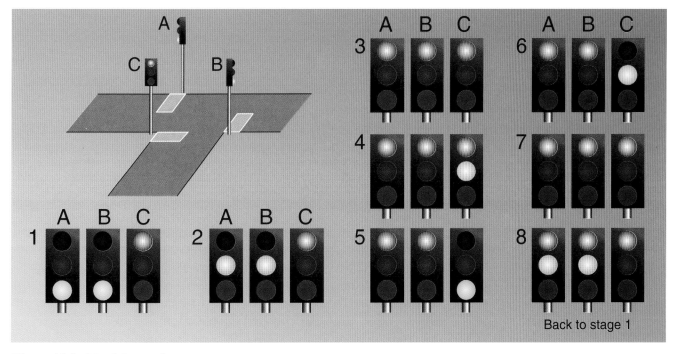

Figure 15.3 *Fixed time cycle.*

The amount of time the lights stay at point 1 and point 5 (Figure 15.3) depends on the plan, and the plan is based on a prediction of the average traffic flow through the junction at that particular time of day. The four plans used in Cleveland are:

▶ Peak a.m.

▶ Off-peak a.m.

▶ Peak p.m.

▶ Off-peak p.m.

The timings used in these plans were worked out using traffic surveys, then the times were programmed into the microprocessors at the junctions. These microprocessors, using the clock built into them, then select the correct plan for the time of day.

PROGRAM CONTROLLED

The third method is computer controlled operation. Since 1985 the traffic lights and pelican crossings in the central areas of both Middlesbrough and Stockton-on-Tees have been controlled between 7 a.m. and 7 p.m. by a central computer sited in one of the County Council's offices in Middlesbrough.

Before we look at how the system operates, we need to see how the area controlled by the system is divided up.

■ How the area is divided up

The whole area covered by the system is split up into regions (as you can see in Figure 15.4). Each region contains a number of junctions. These junctions are called nodes and each one is given a code (for example N27). The nodes are the numbered boxes on the figure. The road between any two nodes in a particular direction is called a link and each link is given a code (like N27C – this shows that it is a link to node 27). At each node there is either a set of traffic lights (which are given a code starting with T – like T004) or a pelican crossing, which is given a code starting with P. There are 42 junctions and 22 pelican crossings under the central computer's control.

On each road leading to a junction (or node) that is controlled using this system, and at some distance from that junction, a detector is buried in the road. Every time a vehicle passes over this detector it sends a signal along a dedicated telephone line to the central computer. The computer knows the state (or colour) of the lights at that time and the average speed of a vehicle between the detector and the junction, and so can calculate the rate of flow of traffic for each road (or link) in and out of that junction.

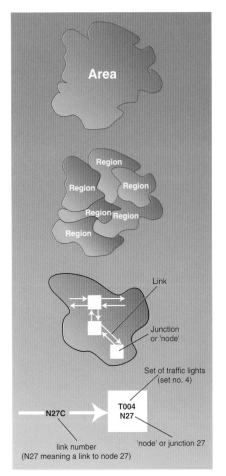

Figure 15.4 How the area is divided up.

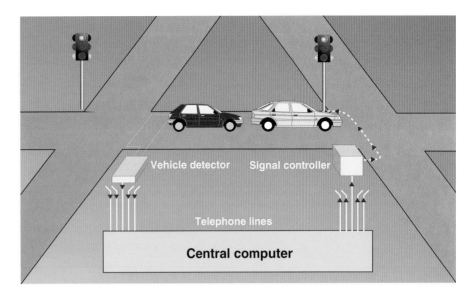

Figure 15.5 *How the system works.*

■ *How the system works*

At any time the state of the flow of traffic (called the 'link congestion') can be displayed on a screen in the control room in the County Council Office.

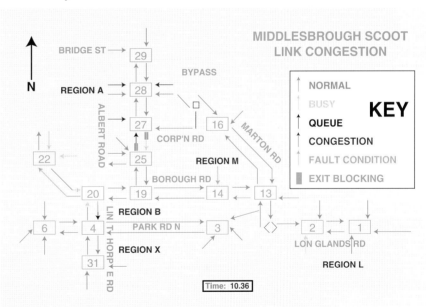

Figure 15.6 *Link congestion for the five regions covering the centre of Middlesbrough.*

Figure 15.6 shows the link congestion for five regions which cover the centre of Middlesbrough. Each node or junction is given a number and has several arrows leading to and from it. The colour of the arrows indicates several things:

▶ Whether the traffic flow is normal (green arrow)

▶ Whether it's busy (yellow)

▶ If there is a queue (black)

▶ If there is congestion (red)

▶ If there is a fault (orange).

If a queue extends from one junction to another, the exit from one of these junctions will be blocked and this shows up on screen as a blue block. The information displayed on the screen is constantly updated.

In Figure 15.6 the flow of traffic through most junctions is normal. One link to node 2 is showing up as busy as are two links to nodes 20 and 22. You can see that the 'busy' flow is in the direction of Region A, which is the most central district of the town.

It is worth looking at node 27 in more detail. Of the four links leading into this junction, two are showing that the flow is normal, a queue is forming in another and there is traffic congestion at the fourth. Only two links lead away from the node – the flow is normal in one and is busy in the other. As node 25 is close to node 27 the busy flow has caused this exit to be blocked at node 27.

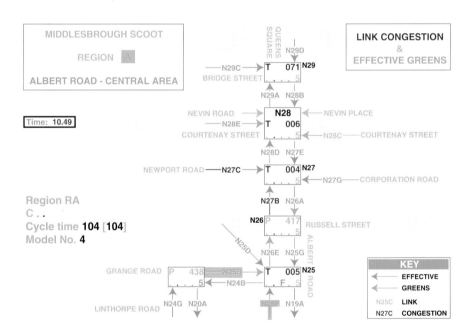

Figure 15.7 *The situation in Region A.*

The traffic controller can display a particular region in more detail (Figure 15.7). This figure displays the situation in Region A 13 minutes later. Each link now shows a code to identify it (for example, N27E), and the colour this code is displayed in indicates the state of the flow (link congestion). The arrows pointing at each node show the condition of the traffic lights, red or green. Now two of the links into node 27 (N27C and N27B) are congested and two (N27G and N27E) are normal.

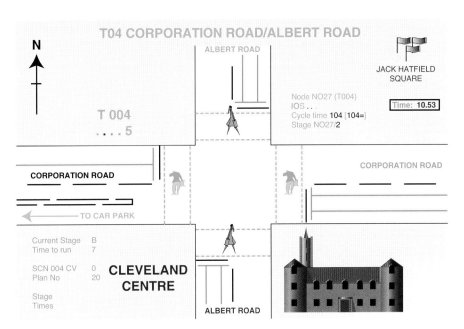

Figure 15.8 *Node 27 with all the lights on red.*

The monitor in the control room can display a particular node instead of a region. Figure 15.8 shows node 27 at a point when all the traffic lights are on red and the crossings at this junction are allowing pedestrians to cross. Figure 15.9 shows the same node at a different point in the cycle – the traffic lights along Albert Road are on green and those on Corporation Road are on red.

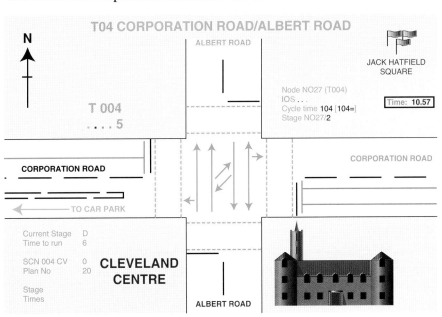

Figure 15.9 *Node 27 at another point in the cycle.*

Although these displays allow the traffic controller to see exactly what is happening in great detail, the computer program (not the controller) actually deals with the problems of congestion. The program takes into account all the data being fed into it, and tries to relieve the queues and congestion by altering, a little at a time, the timings of the lights.

The computer uses a technique called SCOOT (this stands for *S*plit *C*ycle *O*ffset *O*ptimisation *T*echnique), and the program in the central computer can alter the time any light is on a particular colour (the *split*), the time it takes for a set of lights to go through a complete cycle (the *cycle*) and the timings between different nodes (the *offset*). The controller can change the timings manually, but doesn't do it very often, usually only when accidents occur or when there are roadworks in the area.

What happens if the system fails?

If the computer system fails, the traffic lights automatically go back to operating in 'fixed time' mode. If faults occur, the condition shows up on the various screen displays and a buzzer sounds in the control room. These faults are logged by the computer and can be printed out at any time. At 3 a.m. the computer program checks all parts of the system (detectors, lights, etc.) for faults and the results of these tests are logged and printed out so that the engineers can trace any faults and repair them.

Car parking

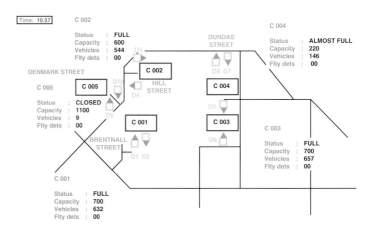

Figure 15.10 Car park monitoring.

This computer system also controls the information signs about car parks in the town centre. Detectors in the road at the entrances and exits of the car parks send signals back to the central computer which can then count the number of vehicles in each car park. The computer also stores the total number of vehicles each car park can accommodate and sends signals to the electronic signs to display each car park's status – whether it has spaces, how full it is or whether it is closed.

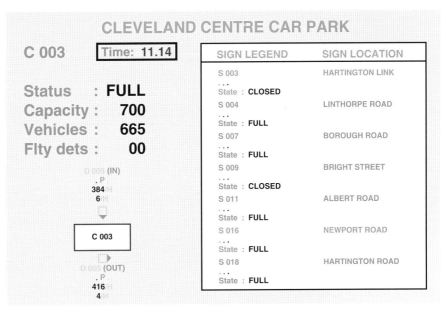

Figure 15.11 *Another display used to monitor car parks.*

Diagrams displayed on the monitor can show the details of all the car parks in an area or details of each car park separately. These displays give the status, the capacity of the car park, the number of vehicles currently parked and the number of faulty detectors. The screen for one particular car park also shows the message that's being displayed on electronic information signs in the area, regarding its state. Exactly what is being displayed on each of these signs can also be shown on the screen.

Figure 15.12 *The screen showing the display on the car park sign.*

The actual sign.

Questions

1 The traffic light system of a large town is to be computerised. The lights at many junctions are to be controlled by a single central computer.

    a Give two types of input required for the system
    b Give two benefits of introducing the system.

SEG specimen paper

16 IT in a Supermarket

Today, IT is vital to the retail business in general, and to supermarkets in particular. In a large modern supermarket computers are used in many different ways, from controlling the stock to controlling the temperatures in fridges and freezers. In this chapter we will take a detailed look at these uses in a large supermarket which is one branch of a national chain.

Our supermarket uses several computers, which are kept in a room called the system office. One of these computers is used to control the stock and is connected to each checkout. We shall call this the 'branch computer'.

Each checkout has an **electronic point of sale** (EPOS) till, and each EPOS till has the following:

▶ a keyboard

▶ a digital display

▶ a scanner to read bar codes

▶ a set of scales

▶ a printer

▶ a credit/debit card reader

▶ a till drawer.

All of these parts are attached to the base unit of every till. The base unit is connected by cables to the branch computer in the system office.

■ *Bar codes*

Every product on sale must have an identifying code number different from that of every other product. Different sizes of the same product need different code numbers as well. These numbers are printed onto the labels or packaging of the product as bar codes (you can see an example of a bar code in Figure 16.1).

A bar code contains four pieces of data:

▶ The code for the country the company producing the product comes from. The code for the UK is 50.

Figure 16.1 *A bar code.*

Q

The bar code for the UK is 50. Find out the codes for

Germany
France
Any other country

Collect some bar codes and try to identify the country code and the company code for each one

Why doesn't the bar code on a tin of soup contain its price?

▶ The code for the company which produces the product – 00314 in the example in Figure 16.1.

▶ The code for the product – 40052 in our example.

▶ A check digit, to make sure that the bar code has been read correctly.

Nearly all grocery products now have a bar code.

■ *Scanners*

The bar codes on products are read by the infrared beam on the scanners at the EPOS till. Scanners come in many different forms. Here are four of them:

▶ wand

▶ gun

▶ horizontal scanner

▶ flat bed scanner.

You can see examples of these in Figure 16.2.

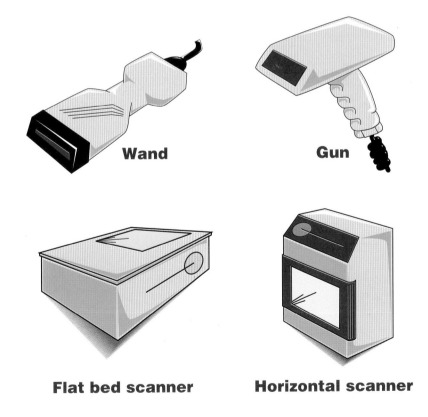

Wand   **Gun**

Flat bed scanner   **Horizontal scanner**

Q

Which two scanning devices would allow bar codes to be read most quickly?

Why?

Figure 16.2 *The types of scanning devices that are used to read bar codes.*

```
          SAVEMORE
   QUALITY AT LOWEST PRICES

                          £
   K/ORA WHOLE ORANGE    2.19
   S PINK T/TISSUE X9     2.49
   S T/TISSUE GRNX9       2.49
   AMB DEVON CUSTARD      0.49
   D/M FRUIT COCKTAIL     0.63
   MANDARINS + SYRUP      0.48
   S P/PEACH SLICES       0.37
   TOMATO JUICE           1.29
   HZ TOMATO KETCHUP      0.74
   S S+V CRNCHY STICK     0.42
   WALLFAN WAFERS         1.09
   C/CLASSIC MINT         0.54
   S MINI PIZZAS X10      1.19
   S MILD CURE HAM        1.55
   S LAMB CUTLETS         1.02
   F/F HAGGIS             2.52
   1.57lb @ £0.59/lb
   APPLES EMPIRE          0.93
   S SALMON               1.65
   HZ TOMATO SOUP         0.32
   HZ TOMATO SOUP         0.32
   HZ TOMATO SOUP         0.32
   HZ TOMATO SOUP         0.32
   WALL VIENNETTA         1.09
   S SZ3 EGGS X18         1.74
   MORN ORN+NUT CRNCH     0.55
   MORN ORN+NUT CRNCH     0.55
   S SIRLOIN STEAK        3.51
   LEMONS LS              0.18
   S MARGARINE            0.75

   ****      TOT         31.73

   CASH                  40.00
   CHANGE                 8.27

   31/05/94  12.28  0667  02 66

        THANK YOU
   FOR SHOPPING WITH SAVEMORE
```

Figure 16.3 *An itemised till receipt.*

This particular supermarket uses flat bed scanners. When an item is passed over the scanner, a sequence of events happens very quickly:

1 It reads the bar code and sends the number it represents to the branch computer.
2 The branch computer uses the number to look up the product record in a file. The record contains the price and a description of the product.
3 This data is sent back to the EPOS till at the checkout.
4 The till shows the item and price on the digital display, prints them on a receipt and adds the price to the total.
5 At the same time the branch computer records what has been sold.

When a bar code has been scanned properly, the scanner makes a beeping sound – if this sound isn't made, the item must be passed over the scanner again until the bar code has been read correctly. The operator uses the keyboard to enter codes of products that won't scan, for example reduced price items.

The scales at the EPOS till are also linked to the branch computer. All loose fruit and vegetables are weighed at the checkout and the product's code number is typed at the keyboard to give the customer a description of the product on the receipt, together with its weight and price (you can see an itemised receipt, containing this sort of information in Figure 16.3).

The printer attached to the EPOS till can print cheques and debit/credit card vouchers as well as printing an itemised receipt. This makes mistakes much less likely, and saves time.

Transferring funds electronically

Many people now choose to pay by credit or debit card rather than cash. The customer's card is passed through the card reader, which reads the data (usually the account number and date of expiry) on the magnetic strip on the back of the card. The data from the magnetic strip of a debit card is then used, together with details of the amount spent, to transfer this amount from the customer's bank account to the supermarket's bank account. This process is called **electronic funds transfer** (**EFT**) and works even if the supermarket's bank and the customer's bank are different.

■ *Stock control*

In fact, two branch computers are linked to the EPOS terminals at the checkout. They both store the data about items sold and act as backup for each other. Imagine what would happen if only one computer was used and it broke down.

These branch computers are linked via telephone lines to a large main computer at the supermarket's head office in another part of the country. The computers at all the branches are linked to the main computer like this.

After the supermarket has closed at the end of the day, the branch computer sends the details of every sale to the main computer at head office. The main computer system uses this data to update the records of the stock of every item in each store. It uses a forecast of sales along with other factors (such as the weather or time of year) to automatically order the correct amount of stock needed by each store for the next day. The main computer also transmits these orders to computers in the distribution centres. These are large warehouses storing products ready for delivery. The distribution centres deliver the stock to the stores immediately.

At the same time as the branch computers send their sales data to the main computer, the main computer sends back any price changes, descriptions of new items and details of any special offers to each branch.

In addition to being used for stock control, the sales data is stored by the main computer at the head office to build up a 'profile' or description of the way its customers shop. For example, the proportion of customers who use powder compared with those who use liquid detergent can be worked out from the sales of washing detergents in any particular store. This sort of information can be used to work out how much shelf space each product should have.

■ *Pricing*

The branch computer holds the price of each product and sends it to the EPOS terminal when the product's bar code is read. The package doesn't show the price, and doesn't have a price label – the only place where the price is displayed is on a label attached to the shelf near the product (like the one in Figure 16.4).

SAVEMORE FRESH TURKEY
5X5LB

£**1.19**
per lb

35881   UPO 5
200090200000 7   9425

Figure 16.4 *The type of shelf label you are likely to see in a supermarket.*

It used to be that every single item had its own price label, which meant that when the price changed new labels had to be stuck on top of the old ones. This took quite a long time to do, as every item on the shelves affected by the price change had to be relabelled, and any mistakes meant that customers would be overcharged or under-charged. Now, when price changes are sent from the head office computer to the branch computer during the night, new shelf labels are printed and the night staff in the supermarket put these on the shelves ready for the next day.

Special offers – like 'Buy two and get one free' or 'Buy one product and save 50% on another' – couldn't be offered easily before the introduction of IT. Now, as the bar codes are scanned, the branch computer looks for items on special offer and discounts the prices where necessary.

Figure 16.5 *A special offer label.*

Freezers and chiller cabinets

Computers are also used to control the freezers and chiller cabinets throughout the store. The large freezers in the warehouse have to be kept within a certain temperature range. This is done using temperature **sensors** inside each freezer to monitor the conditions. Data from these sensors is sent to the computer and it switches the cooling motors on and off.

On the floor of the supermarket many freezers and chiller cabinets are used to store and display a wide variety of products such as fresh meat, dairy produce and frozen goods. Different products need to be stored at different temperatures – fresh meat, for example, may have to be kept at 4°C while ice cream has to be kept at –15°C. In the past, an employee had to check the temperature of each freezer and chiller cabinet every hour. Now they are all linked to a computer in the branch office. A temperature sensor in each freezer and chiller constantly sends data back to the computer, which sends signals back to switch the individual freezer and chiller motors on and off, maintaining the correct temperatures. A display on each cabinet shows the temperature to the customers.

The kind of display you are likely to see on a chiller cabinet.

Freezer and chiller cabinets are a common sight in today's supermarkets.

Each chiller and freezer has to be defrosted every three or four hours, and the computer controls this process. Any breakdowns are detected immediately, which reduces the risk of food thawing and being wasted.

■ *Advantages of IT in a supermarket*

The advantages of using IT in supermarkets can be broken down into two sections:

▶ the benefits to the customers

▶ the benefits to the supermarket management.

Remember that changes and improvements come about over a period of time. While the introduction of IT will eventually save the supermarket chain money, a good deal of investment, both in terms of resources and training, is needed. This does not happen just at the start but throughout the development of the new system.

ADVANTAGES TO THE CUSTOMER

Customers will find that IT makes their shopping easier in many ways.

▶ The checkout services are faster and more efficient.

▶ Till receipts are itemised, so they can check prices and see if any mistakes have been made.

▶ The products are more tailored to their needs.

▶ The goods are fresher because stock levels held by supermarkets can be lower.

▶ There are more special offers.

▶ The benefits to the supermarket are passed on through lower prices or better customer services.

▶ Various methods of payment are allowed, so they don't have to carry cash.

▶ Chilled and frozen foods are kept at the correct temperature, so health hazards are much lower.

ADVANTAGES TO THE SUPERMARKET AND MANAGEMENT

IT also brings a number of advantages to the store management.

▶ Stock control is more efficient, so there is less chance of goods being out of stock.

▶ The checkout is more efficient and there is less chance of staff making errors.

▶ Sales forecasts and profiles can be made, which leads to more efficient use of shelf space.

▶ Little warehouse space is needed in each supermarket because of the efficient distribution system.

▶ The performance of the checkout staff can be monitored.

▶ Shelf pricing is more cost effective than labelling each product separately.

▶ The ability to use electronic funds transfer improves cash flow.

▶ Chilled and frozen goods can be managed effectively.

Questions

1 A supermarket changes over from traditional cash registers to point-of-sale terminals which use bar-code readers. Explain why additional information provided by the new system might worry the checkout operator.

MEG sample material

2 Describe two changes in employment which result from the introduction of computers in the supermarkets.

MEG sample material

3 A bar code is printed on the label of a tin of beans.

    a Give four examples of ways in which a supermarket could make use of this bar code.

    b Name one benefit to the customer of the use of the bar code.

MEG sample material

4 Many supermarkets now use computerised systems to add up sales, produce till receipts and check stock levels.

State two effects these systems have on
    a Shoppers
    b Management
    c Employees

NEAB specimen material

5 Not all shops use computerised systems like the one described in this chapter. Explain why such a system would be unlikely to be used in a small greengrocer's shop.

NEAB specimen material

IT and Society

The introduction of IT on a large scale has had far-reaching effects on society. Some of these have been unpopular, but many have been beneficial. As the effects have caused concerns, laws have been introduced to control the use of data stored in computer-readable form and to deal with theft of and damage to data.

■ *Controlling data use*

The law gives people the right to see any data about themselves which is stored on computer. If the data is wrong they have the right to make sure it is changed or removed from the database.

People and firms that store data about living people have to obey certain rules.

▶ They must make sure the data is collected in a fair way and that it's only used for the purpose for which it was collected. To make sure they don't suddenly invent new purposes they have to register that they are using the data, describing what they will be using it for and how they will get the data. Data collected for a particular purpose must be just what is needed for that purpose. It is not legal to collect lots of data about people when it is not relevant to the task that is going to be carried out.

▶ Once the data has been collected the data user must see that it is kept up to date and when they have finished with it the data must be destroyed.

▶ While the data is stored it must be protected from accidental loss or alteration by keeping backup copies in a safe place. Data must also be protected from deliberate damage or theft so companies using data must have good security systems (such as passwords) to be able to read and alter files. Doors to rooms containing storage media and computer systems must be kept locked. The more sensitive the data is, the more important it is that the protection is effective.

▶ Data can't be given away or sold unless the intention to do this has been registered. Companies who want to sell data can do so without referring to the person concerned as long as they have registered sale of data as one of the things they want to do with it.

Some kinds of data are exempt from some or all of these rules. The contents of word processed documents are completely exempt and so is data from which the subject can't be identified (including data from market research surveys where the person's name isn't stored).

Even when companies work within these rules, some of their activities can annoy some people. A great deal of information is available freely and legally. Sources include:

▶ the electoral register

▶ telephone directories

▶ the Royal Mail database of postal addresses

▶ lists of property valuations for the council tax.

Some of this information is available on paper but quite a lot can be supplied as data in computer-readable form. Individually, these databases may not provide much information but if the data from several is combined then a great deal can be worked out about an individual. Various mail order operators and subscriptions departments of magazines and clubs will sell information on their databases (they get permission to pass on information by asking their customers to indicate if they do not want it passed on to firms selling similar products). **Credit reference agencies** also supply information about a person's ability to repay loans.

With all this data stored in database files, it's quite easy to build up a detailed personal profile on someone. This could include:

▶ name

▶ address

▶ age group (possibly date of birth)

▶ family details

▶ the value of the house they live in

▶ whether they own or rent their home

▶ information on income and credit rating

▶ information on buying habits.

Combining data like this isn't illegal as long as the resulting database is registered, but it's very unlikely that anyone would ever know that a particular firm had all this data on them. To check that the data stored is accurate and up to date a person needs to know who holds the data.

Data from these databases is often sold as lists to companies who want to use **direct mailing** or **telesales** to sell their products. The lists can be selected to include certain types of people – those in a certain age group, or a particular income band, or with a history of buying similar products, for example. Although these uses can be annoying they don't actually do any real harm. But the personal profiles could be used as the basis of discrimination, sometimes on

Q

What rights does the Data Protection Act give to members of the general public?

Data users have to make sure that while the data is stored, it must be protected from accidental loss or alteration. Give one method of achieving this.

How can data be protected against deliberate damage or theft?

The Data Protection Act only covers data stored on computer databases. Write down your views on whether or not the law should be extended to cover paper-based data.

the basis of faulty conclusions from out of date or incorrectly interpreted information.

■ *Hacking*

Hacking is the term used to describe the process of illegally **accessing** and sometimes altering data stored in a computer system. The person who does it is called a **hacker**. Even if they don't damage the data, if a person who has no right to see the data looks at it they are committing a criminal offence. Often, even if there is no intention of damaging the data in the system, data is lost because the hacker handles it wrongly – and sometimes the hacker intends to alter the data. Altering the data can lead to substantial losses to the owner of the data – which is often what the hacker intends to happen. It is very important that data is accurate – in some applications it is vital. Hackers have been known to alter the data in hospital systems and change patient records and prescriptions – luckily, so far, the changes have been detected before any harm was caused.

■ *Data and software theft*

DATA THEFT

Data and programs stored in computer-readable form can be copied quickly without leaving evidence that they have been copied. Data is often valuable and could be very sensitive, so it must be protected from attempts to make illegal copies.

The best way of doing this is to convert the data to a coded form using an **encryption** program. The program alters the data in a complex way so that, without knowing the exact method of encryption, it is impossible to restore the original data. So encrypted data is useless to a thief.

SOFTWARE THEFT

Theft of software is a major problem. People who wouldn't normally dream of committing a crime often make extra copies of computer programs so they can use them on more machines, use them at home, or give them to friends. This means that the author of the program loses income from selling more copies of the program – and it is illegal.

Computer software must be sold in a usable form, so encryption can't be used to protect these programs. Business users also expect to be able to make backup copies of the programs they use (which is legal), so the kind of copy-protection methods often used for computer games can't be used.

Large-scale copying and sale of computer software has been known. These cases have involved both business software and games. Sale of these illegal copies (usually much cheaper than the original program) represents a huge loss to the computer industry.

Software users who steal programs like this are damaging the industry. It takes a long time and costs a lot of money to develop a commercial software package. If the company making such a package doesn't get the income they expect from a program because it is being copied and sold illegally they won't be able to pay for developing new packages.

Summary

- Data stored in computer-readable form can be used in ways not possible with data stored on paper.
- A law has been introduced to control the use of data in computer-readable form.
- Laws have also been introduced to deal with data theft and damage.
- Data has to be collected fairly and lawfully.
- Data stored on computer must be accurate and up to date.
- A person can see the data stored about them and change it if it is wrong.
- Data must only be used for the purpose it was collected for.
- Data must be kept secure.
- Accessing and altering data without the right to do so is a crime.
- Data can be protected by encryption.
- Making extra copies of programs and selling them, using them on additional machines or giving them to friends is a crime.

Questions

1 Personal information is held by various organisations, some of which may concern you or members of your family. Give one example of such an organisation and three items of personal information which you think this organisation might hold about you or your family (other than name and address).

NEAB specimen material

Questions cont'd

2 Banks store information about their customers on computer files.

    a Suggest three items of personal information (other than name and address) which a bank might store on their customers.

    b How might these items of information be misused?

MEG sample material

3 It is possible that some of the personal information held about a customer on a bank's computer file is inaccurate. Discuss the possible consequences of this inaccuracy for the customer.

NEAB specimen material

4 A school stores dates of births of pupils. Give two ways in which it might sensibly use this information.

MEG sample material

5 State three ways in which data held on police computers is used to prevent or detect crime.

MEG sample material

6 The PROFOR group collect information about individuals across the country. They then construct profiles of these individuals. Information about a person is collected from various sources including the electoral register, the Royal Mail database on addresses and postcodes, information on property values based on advertising in local papers, information bought from book clubs and mail order firms and information from credit reference agencies.

    The personal files are stored in a computer database then the database is interrogated to produce lists of people selected according to criteria provided by firms wishing to buy information. Firms use the information to allow them to target direct mailing and telephone canvassing to sell a variety of goods and services.

    Discuss the moral and ethical implications of both the methods used to collect the data and the possible use of the profiles produced. (Credit will be given for organisation and presentation of your answer as well as for its content.)

NEAB specimen material

7 Describe how a computer hacker might do more harm than an office burglar.

MEG sample material

8 Describe two features of computer storage of data which might make its misuse more serious than misuse of the same data stored in a filing cabinet.

MEG sample material

9 Give two examples where the transfer of information from one computer system to another is beneficial to the public.

MEG sample material

10 There are many ways in which computers help newspaper reporters to prepare text for presentation to the printer.

Questions cont'd

a Describe two such ways that have been used.

b Describe how the job of a newspaper reporter has changed through developments in information technology.

MEG sample material

11 A computer holds false information about you. Give an example of one trivial error in the information and one more serious mistake. In each case describe a possible serious consequence and a method of avoiding the problem.

MEG sample material

12 Discuss the extent to which governments should encourage firms to use IT if unemployment is a consequence.

MEG sample material

13 There are many situations other than at school where you might find computers. Name three such situations and give one reason for using computers in each of these places.

For one of these places, give examples in which using computers makes it easier for a person working there.

MEG sample material

14 A video hire shop uses a database to keep information on the videos that it lends out. Explain the meanings of the following database terms using the example given above in your answer.

a a field

b a file

MEG sample material

c a record.

Glossary of terms used in the text

accessing Reading data from a computer file, or writing data to a computer file

algorithm A plan showing the steps needed to solve a problem or carry out a task

analogue (value) A quantity which varies continuously, without fixed gaps between values. An example is temperature

aural (information) Information which is heard

backup copy A copy of computer-readable data stored on a separate disk or tape, to be used if the original is lost or damaged

backing store The disk, tape or other medium used to hold computer-readable data. Data stored here is not lost when the computer is switched off

binary number A number consisting only of ones and zeros

blocks (of text) A portion of a document which is marked and then handled as a single unit

boundaries (of a system) The limits of a system. A statement of what the system will do and what it will not do

buffer box An interface used to connect sensors to a computer

calibrate (a sensor) To match readings from a sensor to an accepted scale in known units

CD-ROM An optical disk used to store a large amount of computer-readable data. The data can be read but not changed

cell A single box or location in a spreadsheet

cell address The column letter and row number which identify a particular box in a spreadsheet

centre (text) To place text symmetrically between the left and right margins, for example in a word processed document

changing margins To change the amount of space left at the edges of a document. If text is already present it will be rearranged

charting package A package designed to produce graphs and charts from data entered by the user

chip An electronic circuit, on a small slice of silicon, designed to do a particular job

clip-art Ready-made pictures and diagrams, stored on disk, which can be used to illustrate documents

column width The number of characters that can be fitted in the cells in a column of a spreadsheet

computer aided design (CAD) package A software package for producing detailed technical plans and drawings, and for doing calculations

constraint (in a system) Limits imposed in system design – such as cost limits, availability of hardware and software

context The situation in which data becomes information

copy (a disk or file) To duplicate the computer-readable data onto another disk

corruption (of a disk or file) Altering data so it is either unusable or unreadable

credit reference agency A firm which keeps records about the financial status of people, to supply information to others

cursor A small box, arrow, line or cross which shows the current position on the screen

data Information removed from its context and encoded for computer use

data-logging collecting and storing data at regular, fixed intervals over a period of time

database A collection of files which can be searched or processed in a variety of ways to produce different outputs

database report The printed output from a database

deleting (text) Removing unwanted text from a document

desktop publishing (DTP) Page layout software which allows text and graphics to be combined in a variety of ways

digital Consisting of distinct numbers

direct mailing Advertising by sending letters straight to people, without having been asked to supply information

distorting (sounds) Adding noise, or altering the length of a sound to change it in some way

document A letter, report or other piece of work produced using a word processing package

document template Standard settings for documents. These can be saved on disk and re-used

documentation Written information about a computer system. It is usually divided into **user documentation** and **maintenance documentation**

documenting Writing the user and maintenance instructions for a computer system

double spacing Leaving a blank line between lines of text in a document

drawing package A package used to produce line drawings. It handles each piece of the drawing as a separate object

duplicate (part of a drawing) Automatically producing multiple copies of an object or group of objects in a drawing

EFT Electronic funds transfer, used to transfer money between accounts immediately

EPOS Electronic point of sale system, used in shops to read bar codes and look up prices, often linked to stock control systems

encryption Altering data stored on disk or transmitted from one computer to another so that it makes no sense if it is stolen

end-user The person who will eventually use an information technology system

error trapping Detecting and handling data that's been input wrongly in a way which allows the computer program to continue to run

evaluate (software) Deciding how well a software package carries out a given task

feedback Continuous use of data from sensors to control the output of a computer system

field A single data item in a record

field length The number of characters that can be fitted into a field

field type The kind of data which can be stored, for example numbers, characters, true/false

file A collection of related records

file format The way data in a file is stored on disk

fill (a shape) To colour in the inside of a drawing on the screen with a selected shade

format (of a spreadsheet cell) The way the data in the cell is displayed

formula The method for carrying out calculations in a spreadsheet. The formula contains the addresses of cells used in doing the calculation

frame A rectangular shape used in DTP packages. Text or graphics can be placed in it and the frame and contents are handled as a single object

full justification Spacing is adjusted so that the text is spread out to fill a whole line, so both left and right edges of the text make straight lines

function (in a spreadsheet) A predefined method of carrying out a calculation – for example working out an average

grading (a fill) Altering the shade of the filling colour from light to dark. This can make objects look more curved or three-dimensional

graphics Any kind of drawings or charts included in a document, or produced on their own

group (of objects) Several objects, in a drawing, which are collected together and linked so that they can be handled as if they were just one thing

hacker A person who makes illegal access to a computer system

hacking The process of gaining illegal access to a computer system

heading area The area of a database report containing data which is printed at the top of each page of the report

icon A small picture representing an action available to the user of a package. Icons are selected using a mouse

implementing Setting up a computer system and ensuring that it runs properly

importing (data/files) Loading data, or whole files, produced using one software package, into another software package

information Data placed in a context so that it has meaning

information retrieval Getting data out of computer-readable files and putting it into context so that it can be understood by users

inserting (text) Adding extra text into a word processed document

integrated package A set of programs, usually including a word processor, a spreadsheet and a database, designed so that data can be moved easily between the different sections

interface unit A piece of hardware which allows communication between a computer and devices such as sensors attached to it

justification The way text or other data is arranged in the space available

landscape orientation Arranging the page layout so that the document is short and wide

layer (of a drawing) One level in the drawing. The objects drawn at this level can be moved so that they are in front of or behind things drawn on different levels

left justification Arranging the contents of a line of text, or other data, so that the left edge is straight. The right-hand edge is not straight

line spacing The amount of space left between lines of text. Single spacing leaves less space than double spacing

LOGO A computer programming language with commands which can be used to control movement of a screen turtle or of an external device

magnetic disk A thin, circular piece of metal or plastic, coated with a material which can be magnetised. Data is stored by magnetising tiny spots in different directions

magnetic tape A long thin strip of plastic tape, coated with a material which can be magnetised. Data is stored as magnetised spots arranged across the tape

mail merging Taking data from a file and inserting it into a word-processed document. Can be used to send the same letter to lots of different people

maintenance documentation A description of how a computer system has been set up. This will provide information so that alterations or additions to the system can be made easily

margins The positions at which lines of text start and end

MIDI interface The industry standard method of connecting instruments such as keyboards to a computer system

mixing (sounds) Combining different sounds so that they are played at the same time, producing a composite sound

mouse A device attached to the computer by a cable, and moved across a mat. The movement rolls a ball inside the mouse and this movement is translated into movement of a pointer on the screen. Selection is by clicking one of the buttons on the mouse

moving blocks (of text) Selecting a whole section of text which is cut out of the document and then inserted somewhere else

multimedia Using sound, pictures, text (and often animated sequences) to communicate information

object A part of a drawing or page which is handled as if it is a single item

optical disk A disk which uses light to store and retrieve data

page template The layout to be used for all the pages in a document, stored as a file

painting package A package used to produce pictures. The computer stores the colour of each pixel, altering the size of sections is difficult

password A word, or number, which has to be typed into the computer system in order to gain access to programs or data

password hierarchy A system of passwords, giving different levels of access to programs and data

peripheral device A piece of hardware (such as a printer or a sensor) which is connected to a computer

pitch (of a sound) How high or low a sound is

pixel One spot on a computer screen which can be illuminated in a particular colour or left black

portrait orientation Arranging the layout of a page so that the document is tall and narrow

primary key field A database field in which each value is unique, allowing an individual record to be found easily

printing (files) Sending data to a printer to produce output on paper

procedure A set of instructions within a computer program, to carry out a particular task. Each procedure has a name and the task can be carried out using this name

processing stage In a computerised system, this is a stage where data is used or altered in some way

program A set of instructions, in the correct order, which cause the computer to carry out a particular task

programming language The words and phrases that can be used in writing a computer program make up a programming language

query A method used to search a database for records which have certain things in common

range (of numbers) Numbers between a known minimum value and a known maximum value

range (of cells) All the cells in a spreadsheet that lie within an area between two specified cell addresses

real-time A computer application in which input data is processed quickly enough for this data to affect the output from the system

record A record contains data about one person or thing. It is divided into fields

record area The part of a database report which contains data for each record selected for printing

report The printed output from a database system

report format The layout of a database report

resolution The number of separate points which can be displayed on a computer screen

right justification Arrangement of text, or other data, so that the right hand edge makes a straight line down the page. The left hand edge is not even

sampling (sound) Storing sound data so that it can be played back using the stored data

sampling interval   The time between taking samples of data

saving (files)   Storing data on a disk or tape so that it can be reloaded later

scan   To detect the pattern of light and dark, or different colours, on a page and transmit the data to a computer where it is used to produce a screen image

scanner   A device which produces a scan by detecting the amount of light reflected from each point on a page

search (a database)   To find all the records in the database which have the required values in certain fields

selecting (records)   Marking particular records so that an action applies to all of them. Often done by searching

selecting (blocks of text)   Indicating the beginning and end of a section of text which can then be handled using block commands

sensor   A device which detects the state of an environmental condition (such as temperature) and transmits a signal to an interface unit connected to the computer

sequencing (sounds)   Playing back stored sound samples in a particular order

simulation   Using a computer model to predict the outcome of particular events. Sometimes connected to realistic sound, visual and motion effects

single spacing   Printing text with no extra space between text lines

spreadsheet   A grid of boxes or cells, containing data or formulae, which is used to carry out calculations

story   A complete section of text for use by a DTP package

summary area   The part of a database report containing data which will only be printed at the end of the final page of the report

system flowchart   A diagram showing how data moves through a system

system specification   A detailed list of all the tasks a computerised system must be able to carry out, together with any other requirements such as time limits, and amount of data to be stored

tabs   Column positions which can be set as required across a word-processed page

telemetry   Transmission of data from sensors to a receiving station at a distance

telesales   Selling goods by telephoning potential customers

testing plan   A method designed to test a computer system to make sure it works as it should

text editor   A simple package used to produce text files. It provides only basic facilities for entering, editing, and saving text

text file   A file containing only text. Text files are usually produced using text editors or word processors

underlining   Putting a line under a section of text when it is printed

user documentation   All the information provided on paper for the user of a computer system

user guide   Written instructions telling a person how to use a computer system

variable   Something which can change and have different values.

white space   Areas of a page not taken up by text or graphics

word processor   A computer program designed to allow entry, editing, storage and retrieval, and printing, of text

zoom   To enlarge a section of a drawing to allow more detail to be included

Index

Acknowledgements

Thanks are due to the following people who gave their time and help in writing the book:

Mr A. Hill and Mr B. Robinson of Cleveland Educational Computer Centre (CECC), a medical practice in north-east England, the Urban Traffic Control Department of Cleveland County Council, and Mr M. Woods.

The authors and publishers would like to thank the following companies, individuals and institutions who gave permission to reproduce photographs in this book:

Economatics (91, 96 top, 97) with particular thanks to Nick Swift and Kate Ryan; Eye Ubiquitous/L. Fordyce (7); Hank Morgan/ Science Photo Library (96 bottom); James King-Holmes /Science Photo Library (87 both); Lego Dacta UK Ltd (99); Philippe Goutier/Impact (33, 66); Philippe Plailly/Science Photo Library (98); Roger Ressmeyer/Science Photo Library (89); Ronald Grant Archive (32 both); Takeshi Takahara/Science Photo Library (88); Trevor Clifford Photography (9 left, 44, 50, 57, 60, 63, 66, 108, 143 left) with special thanks to UCM, Hove for their assistance; Zefa (5).

We would also like to thank the following bodies who gave permission to reproduce copyright question material:

Southern Examining Group, University of London Examinations and Assessment Council, Midland Examining Group, Northern Examinations and Assessment Board.

The pages were designed by Graphic Designer, Fiona Webb.

The illustrations were produced by GDN Associates. They were drawn using an Apple Macintosh Performa 630 and a Power Macintosh 7100, and the following software - Quark Xpress 3.3, ClarisWorks 2.1, Adobe Illustrator 5.5 and Adobe Photoshop 3.0.

The clip-art on page 51 was reproduced with the permission of the Microsoft Corporation.